# ELEMENTS OF
# ARCHITECTURE

ROB KRIER, SCULPTURE

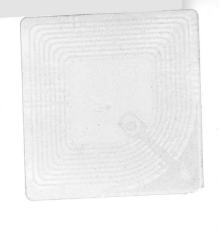

CW00956273

*The most obvious, perhaps even the most archaic, building technique is to lay stone and thus to form an homogeneous constructed mass. A long wall must either be thick enough to stand alone or it needs to be supported by a system of pillars, ribs and terracing, outer covering or network.*

# THE COLUMN

*In a miraculous filigree nature has left us a magnificent encyclopedia of possibilities which could be exploited in building.*
*For thousands of years the basic forms of architecture have been given significant interpretation in stone. The modelling of the shaft,*
*the base and the capital with their complex visual and structural requirements has matured to perfection over the course of time.*

# THE HOUSE

*The enclosing and protecting wall, the differentiation of rooms inside, windows as sources of light, doors as entrances and exits, the roof to keep out the rain and cold . . . all this, thematically, technically or in the architectural aesthetic need no longer be questioned today. Following the destruction of a deep-rooted tradition in the twenties, we must start again, learning to build from the fundamentals.*

*The geometry of the single house derives its force from the contrast with living nature. The greater the density and the number of houses, the greater the displacement of nature and the environment and thus the more important the artificial spaces become. Streets and squares are the vehicles of public life, while quiet cells in the form of courtyards are places of refuge, intimacy and retreat.*

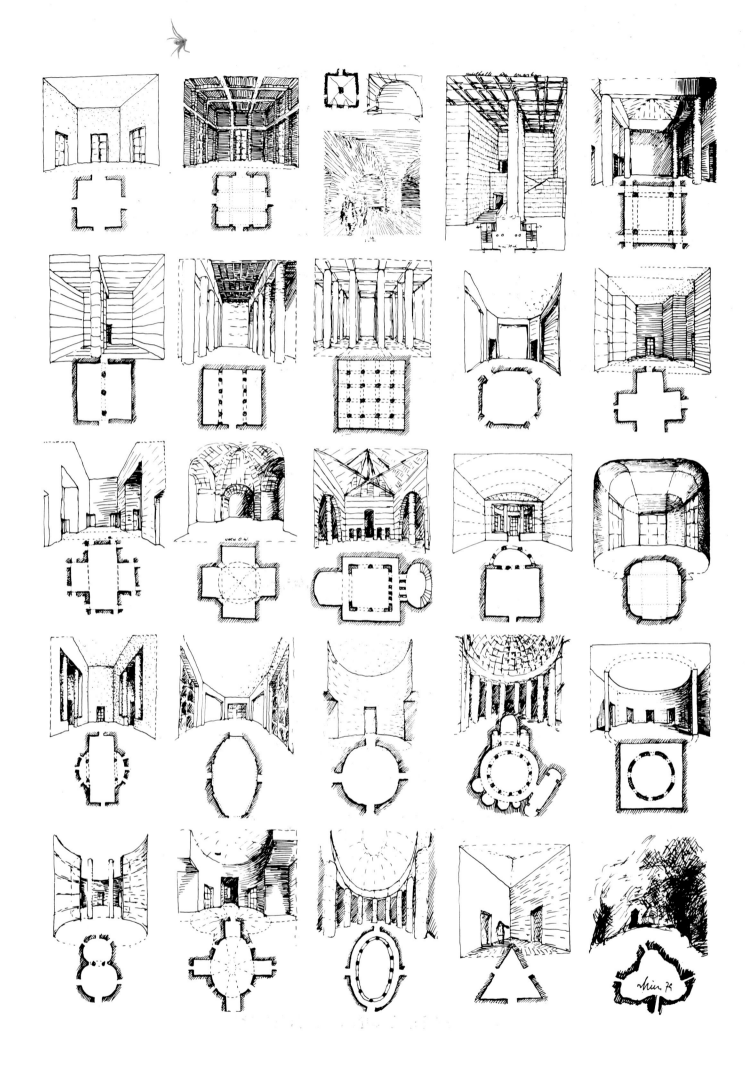

Architectural Design
*Edited by* Andreas C Papadakis

# ELEMENTS OF ARCHITECTURE
## Rob Krier

*ABOVE:* 'THE GREAT VARIETY OF ARCHITECTURE IN THE CITY HAS ALWAYS
BEEN TO ITS ENRICHMENT'; *OPPOSITE:* TYPOLOGICAL SKETCHES

ACADEMY EDITIONS • LONDON

EDITOR

Dr Andreas C Papadakis

First published in Great Britain in 1983 by *Architectural Design* an imprint of the
ACADEMY GROUP LTD, 42 LEINSTER GARDENS, LONDON W2 3AN

Distributed to the trade in the United States of America by
ST MARTIN'S PRESS, 175 FIFTH AVENUE, NEW YORK, NY 10010

ISBN: 1 85490 177 X

AD Profile 49 is published as part of *Architectural Design* Volume 53 9/10-1983

Translated from the German by Romana Schneider. Original text prepared for publication by Deitmar Steiner.
Photographs illustrating the Elements of Architecture by Johann Kräftner unless otherwise credited.

*Front and back cover:* Typological studies of rectangular buildings and U-types and towers by Rob Krier.
*Inside front and back cover:* Student drawings of the interior of the Post Office Savings Bank, Vienna by Otto Wagner
and the staircase of the Art History Museum, Vienna by G Semper and KV Hasenauer.

Printed and bound in Singapore

# CONTENTS

THE OCTAGONAL LIVING ROOM, HOUSE
AT LINDENUFER N-31, BERLIN SPANDAU, 1979

ARCHITECTURAL DESIGN PROFILE No 49

# ELEMENTS OF ARCHITECTURE

## ROB KRIER

Introduction by Andreas Papadakis and Kenneth Powell  11
A Criticism of Modern Architecture
or About the Downfall of the Art of Building  12

ELEMENTS OF ARCHITECTURE  25

ELEMENTS I: INTERIORS  26
The Typology of Interior Spaces  26  The Art of Composing Spaces  36
Ceiling and Floors  40  Columns and Piers  44  Doors  46
Windows  49  Staircases  55

ELEMENTS II: FACADES  60
Entrances and Portals  69  Arcades  70  Ground Floors  71
Bay-Windows, Balconies and Loggias  72  Roofs and Attic Storeys  74

ELEMENTS III: GROUND-PLAN AND BUILDING FORM  76
Square Buildings  78  Rectangular Buildings  81  T-Shaped Ground Plans  82
L-Types  85  U-Types  85  Building Corners  86
Interior Courtyards  90  Outside Staircases  92
Prospect  94  Towers and Monuments  94

The Market Place in Karlsruhe looking towards the Palace

The Circus in Karlsruhe

# FOREWORD

# To the Second Edition

It is with great pride that we are reissuing the *Elements of Architecture* by Rob Krier. When this issue of *Architectural Design* was first published in 1983 it was an instant success with both students and academics and quickly became a set text for a number of architecture courses throughout the world.

This was the first part to be published of Rob Krier's book *Architectural Composition*. When the whole work appeared a few years later it was received equally enthusiastically. In the words of one reviewer, 'It is, in its way, a masterpiece . . . It is an immensely rich resource book, not merely for use in architectural education as Krier himself suggests, but as an inspired series of lessons in good architectural design'.

It is a great pleasure for us to reprint this issue and to take the opportunity to include eight of Krier's magnificent colour drawings including the *Wall*, the *Column*, the *House* and the *City*.

Rob Krier is a theorist and an architect committed to seeking out fundamental architectural truths. His analysis of traditional architectural form is set in the context of present-day needs. He cuts through many of the simplistic fallacies that lie behind modern architectural criticism and reveals how the architectural agenda remains constant. By severing architecture's association with changing fashion he shows how it responds to the basic human requirements which are unfulfilled by design alone, while remaining a vital medium to communicate the most significant social and spiritual values.

Krier does not fit readily into any of the contemporary stylistic categories, though his traditionalism is, in some ways, deep and sincere. He is a definite eclectic, whose view of 'tradition' is original and far from static. He looks at tradition not as a static quantity, anchoring humanity to the past, but as a measure of the present. Krier's analysis of traditional architectural form is set in the context of present-day needs – he is not a simple reactionary – but looks beyond them.

The essence of Krier's work is to be sought in his deep belief in the power of beauty and order – not an artificially imposed, authoritarian order but that order which is part of the power of nature in the world. He reflects the Modern Movement's attempt to redefine the image of a church, a house or a museum and restores the place of symbolism, a guiding force through history.

Krier is not just a theorist. His buildings are at one with his theory, demonstrations of the power of tradition in the face of what he sees as an anarchic and destructive sabotage of ancient values. His influence on architectural design in the years since this book first appeared has been immense and does not look set to diminish. In times of confusion and decay, as well as of rebirth and creativity, Krier reasserts constant values. He is a true humanist who, like the artists and philosophers of the Renaissance, does not reject the past but looks to it to instruct and inspire the future.

*Andreas Papadakis*

# A Criticism of Modern Architecture
# or About the Downfall of the Art of Building

*This essay, and the typological studies of the elements of architecture which follow, are extracted from Rob Krier's magnum opus,* Architectural Composition, *currently being prepared for publication by Academy Editions (see page 88 for details). This 'critical and admonishing' essay, in Krier's own words, 'should serve as a logical link, connecting analytic and applied theory, and it should be critical in order to selectively filter the achievements in architecture of half a century, to examine what they represent.' The typologies and the accompanying examples of student work were made over a period of years during course work at the Technical University in Vienna, where Rob Krier has been Professor of Architecture since 1975. Architectural Design is pleased and proud to be able to publish these extracts from what it considers will be one of the most important works of architectural theory of the twentieth century.*

I do not intend to put certain personalities on trial, or to produce a lexical review with the aim of analysing every architectural contribution on the basis of its theoretical stability. What I want to do is to take a good look at architectural tendencies which, widely supported, have influenced whole decades; further, I wish to separate theoretical substance from fashionable trends, and to formulate propositions according to my own personal conviction. These will allow me to make a critical statement, and to give an outlook on an architecture which outlasts the present.

Modern architecture, in a disastrous way, has ruined cities throughout the whole world. The loss of spatiality in the modern city is most especially deplorable. Some years ago, I published a book on this traumatic issue in which I tried to fathom the reason for this destruction.* Spatial urban systems have been radically and callously ignored, while the repertoire of architectural composition has been degraded just as brutally, to become the most primitive formulae; and all this with poor economic and technical 'reasons'.

This development took place with the euphoric support of the entire

* *Urban Space*, Academy Editions, 1979

professional world which finally, during the time of the post-Second World War building boom, saw the chance to realise the architectural revolution dreamt of in the Twenties. The principles of the CIAM Athens Charter, which concerned the separation of functions in the city (zoning), were incorporated into building law at an international level and carried out with the rigour and scrupulousness of bureaucratic machines. This deplorable state of affairs was primarily helped by the indescribable misery in Europe after the Second World War. But oddly enough, in Warsaw for instance, where the situation was worst, areas in ruins which were important for the city's identity were rebuilt with a heroic certainty. Of course this operation was criticised by some people as producing merely stage-sets. Yet the Polish people had been disgraced without being at fault. They therefore made Warsaw a symbol of their national strength. Our modern cities and their buildings are merely functional objects, without any ethical meaning. They are simply production areas or housing estates which people occupy avidly but leave without sorrow, because ugliness sooner or later creates contempt and disgust in every human being, and sometimes leads to delinquency.

The mass housing shortage was abused by speculators in order for them to become rich in a short period of time. The profit-seeking attitude of these people forced the building industry into the use of prefabricated systems and certain other materials regardless of their durability. The planners, as if struck by madness, agreed to this profiteering: by building extremely densely, they made it even easier for building companies to make fast money—a vicious circle, still rotating, but now conscious of its limits. Some planners even welcome the consumer/disposable ideology as a substitute for non-existent architectural concepts.

*The revolution of modern architecture has failed.* Even if it is difficult for professionals to admit this fact, for years journalists and lay-people have been heaping reproaches on us and have given us the most appalling reports. Citizens' initiatives, more than before, vehemently take up urban design problems. The press spies out and hunts down, with more and more success, the dubious operations

Piazza Navona, Rome

Gropius-Stadt, Berlin

Bombed street in Warsaw

The same street after reconstruction

of big building companies.

Industrialisation has not lead to the perfection and reduction in price of building components as it was expected by Le Corbusier and his generation. All that has been achieved is that through mechanization, the architectural detail has been submitted to the laws of production technology. Of course the calculation of the maximum yield simplifies the constructional solution. Also, reducing production time often offends against all practical reasoning. Decadence in architecture and the ruin of building craftsmanship go together, and can only recover together.

Yet I have hope that, despite the discredit architects and the building industry have brought upon themselves by their own faults, there might be a chance for a 'renewal'.

Mankind in our century continues to demonstrate its apocalyptic destructive power. The brutality of self-slaughter is reflected in all parts of industrialised society. The architectural problem that worries me is no doubt one of the most obvious, but certainly not the most threatening problem the twentieth century has given birth to. The architectural problem will neither explode nor emit fatal radiation. But the illnesses which may be created by chemicals which new buildings are stuffed with, I hardly dare to foresee. We wait with distrust and desperation for the results of all these experiments which have plunged us into a meaningless venture.

Of course the individual case does not matter so much, but a host of bad architecture becomes threatening. A few ugly buildings would not be that serious a threat, but if they spread so that in the end hardly one per cent of real quality is left in building activities, then the

time would have come to sit up and take notice.

Unfortunately this ugliness, this private kitsch, in millions of variations flooding city boundaries and countryside in the form of single family houses, is not viewed that way by their inhabitants, as it is the case with their standard upholstered furniture and wall decorations. Education, which at one time everyone enjoyed, has suffocated under empty aestheticism. A society, wealthier and better schooled than ever before, is in danger of wasting away because of its selfishness, which is often accompanied by ridiculous gestures. In philosophical terms, this development seems to represent a logical result. In historical terms it is certainly not the only example of this kind of development. But the decadence in culture to which I refer is by no means confined to the private sector; it is even more obvious in these gigantic, hypertrophic building complexes. Aristocratic power was successfully fought against, and when it finally ceased to exist, we were indeed left with an immensely lavish but tasteful heritage. If the modern bureaucratic and technocratic power structures were taken by storm what would then be left? Only a gigantic rubbish heap of useless equipment and, of course, a scorched earth.

Can we, with good conscience, enter into a heritage of such dubious value? Who would be willing to take over all this hideousness; who would further enjoy all these shapeless idylls?

I think we will put the 'throw-away' ideology into practice and pull down all the rubbish. This would be necessary anyway for economic reasons.

Such is the sad starting-point of contemporary architecture. He who has not yet realised this should open his eyes and name me

Computer Centre, Vienna

Bourgeois dining room in the 'international moderne' style

the modern buildings in his close vicinity which will go down in building history for having met high architectural demands. I live in the centre of a metropolis called Vienna. If I think about the banalities which for the last 30 years have emerged from a ground that is pregnant with tradition, I am on the verge of tears. The illustrations which accompany this essay have been deliberately picked from anonymous modern architecture to be found in all our cities. I am convinced that many lay-people consider these examples as serious contemporary architecture. After all, similar criteria are applied when, from a holiday catalogue, somebody makes a decision about his 'seaside hotel'. What then should one be guided by? In case of doubt, certainly by the buildings which are close to the heart of the ruling parties; in Vienna these would be the UN-City, the Allgemeine Krankenhaus (hospital), the Franz-Joseph railway station or the Hilton Hotel, which is also frequented by Willy Brandt. What also gives certainty is the taste of big companies and banks which, by way of trendy architects, try to pep up their image and, indirectly, their products and services. So it is that lay-people are spell-bound and terrorized by the taste of magnates, who abuse architecture for their own publicity and to be celebrated publicly as cultural patrons.

As an example of how evident the opportunism of powerful clients and architects can be nowadays, I would like to mention two building programmes in Vienna concerning the Ballhausplatz and Schwarzenbergplatz, which have become political issues. After their first glass-facade designs had been successfully rejected by local initiatives, architects and clients changed their attitude and architectural sytle, proposing for the two sites buildings with historicist facades. Nobody knows whether these games were an attempt to deceive the citizens, or whether they were meant to be an ironical affront. The architects concerned, being among the busiest in Vienna, are experienced tradesmen and entrepreneurs. They are too clever not to have a precise strategy for these kinds of prestige objects. Anyway, different groups got very concerned about the architectural tradition of Vienna and initiated meetings and panel discussions, certainly to the amusement of their supposed enemies. These 'enemies' however, veered round to go the 'alternative way': the citizens were invited to discuss proposals, to reject or agree, their choices being manipulated according to the strategy of clients and architects. These 'link' (left) tactics for the fooling of citizens are disgraceful. Architecture has been degraded to a masque, which changes according to a required role in a strategy. It was characteristic of the ensuing discussion that the plans were never dealt with. Only the facades were discussed. Later it become apparent that the former did not exist at all. The 'Mother of the Arts' must have gone astray in a brothel. She has fallen to the market value of a car-body. If this is not capable of being changed abruptly we could end this chapter with some lascivious swear-words, and could better devote our time to a good game of golf.

So much for the 'atmospherical'. Now we can begin our analysis with a relaxed and enlightened mind.

At the beginning of this century, the revolt against traditional architecture took place in several stages and with different shades of opinion.

The garden city movement fought against the overgrowing of the city. Art Nouveau, Vienna Secession or artists and architects like Antoni Gaudí, Tony Garnier, Otto Wagner, Josef Hoffman, Adolf Loos, Henry van de Velde, and many others, attempted successfully to halt the industrialised historicism of the nineteenth century.

At the moment I live in an apartment block typical of the last century, and enjoy the room heights and the cross-section of the three front rooms. But everything which lies behind this front is not worth mentioning, although the flat is 27 metres deep. Twelve metres in front of my window is a facade which could be ours, decorated with this successful industrial ornamentation in Neo-Classical style, exchangeable, but more bearable than an aluminium-profile facade.

Modern alpine hotel architecture, Salzburg, 'accommodating Nature'

Vienna, building by Staber ' ...following closely Fischer von Erlach, Otto Wagner and Loos... ' (quotation by the architect about his building)

Rudolf Hospital, Vienna

Franz-Joseph Railway Station, Vienna, by Schwanzer and Hlaweniczka

Street in Vienna, late nineteenth century

Glasgow School of Art by C.R. Mackintosh, 1897—1909

Casa Milà, Barcelona, by A. Gaudí, 1905—10

All this of course does not reach the level of architecture. The young artists and architects of the nineteenth century detested this kind of work for which the busy plasterers were in demand, and intended to put an end to such activities. They were seeking forms and themes which would be good enough to take the place of the classical styles such as the Romanesque, the Gothic, the Renaissance, the Baroque and Neo-Classicism, which in the nineteenth century were employed arbitrarily.

Mackintosh achieved this liberation by taking refuge in geometry. He did without classical symbols and relied on the aesthetic values inherent in well-proportioned forms, surfaces and structures. The traditional way of composing the building body and its interior were not questioned by him. His conception became very influential for architectural development in the twentieth century.

With Gaudí, the liberation from the classical language happens almost like a sensuous eruption. The sculptural quality of his architecture can be solely attributed to the artist Gaudí. His individual play with interpretations is too irrational to set a precedent. Where his architecture was taken as an example, the results were often awkward *faux pas*. Still, straight-forward geometry is also a good protection for mediocre architects. The realm of irregular design can only be mastered by extremely talented artists.

This may be a warning to all those young architects who think that the spontaneous individual line and liberation from geometry are the pre-conditions for becoming an artistic personality.

The Casa Mila, this immensely powerful architectural event, just cannot be repeated at every corner. It is a unique building. The analysis of the Casa Mila, a steel-structured building on a free plan with a sculpted sandstone facing, reveals a very interesting building type which was only possible because of new technology. But this is a specific quality which was certainly not exploited superficially by Gaudí. Even if he had had to use a traditional solid structure, a similar effect would have resulted. The passion for constructional subtleties is deeply rooted in the Catalan building tradition, and Gaudí certainly benefited from this background.

Whoever builds up and teaches an architectural theory must examine every theorem in terms of its universality. This means that the margin of possible interpretations of principles has to be anticipated, and all tangible experiences in history have to be reviewed for practical application. Thus, only solid principles remain a matter for instruction in order to guarantee sound high quality of work. The truly great artists have indeed a command of this alphabet, but they are also aware of its limits. With their secure instincts, they only abandon approved rules once, after a long search, they have found a yet unknown variant.

The Art Nouveau movement was an international revolt against the historical styles being trivialised. The classical decorative elements were replaced by floral and other ornaments borrowed from nature. But although the results were fresh, powerful and often effusive, as best seen in the works of Horta, van de Velde and Guimard, they were too individual in their interpretation and therefore could not last for long.

The artists of the Vienna Secession led by Otto Wagner, Hoffman, Plecnik etc. had essentially a more classical attitude and abstained from expressionist gestures. Wagner's Post Office Savings Bank in Vienna and Hoffmann's Palais Stoclet in Brussels are wonderful highlights of this movement. Where Hoffman still formally celebrates the detail, Wagner exposes the constructive and technical qualities of the building's parts. Because of the numerous engineering buildings he executed for the 'Stadtbahn' network and the Donaukanal, his attention was drawn on the design qualities of unmasked constructive details. The banking hall of the Post Office Savings Bank is designed with great technical precision as glass-steel architecture, which until then was only applied to halls and greenhouses.

Casa Batlló, Barcelona, by A. Gaudí, 1904—06

Métro station, Paris, by H. Guimard, 1899—1900

Palais Stoclet, Brussels, by J. Hoffmann, 1905—11

Maison du Peuple, Brussels, by V. Horta, 1896—99

Road bridge over the river Norderelbe by Meyers, Hauers and Pieper, 1884—88

Water Tower, Hamburg, by von Lindley and de Chateauneuf, 1854

Building at Michaelerplatz, Vienna, by A. Loos, 1910

Competition design for the Chicago Tribune by A. Loos, 1922

In retrospect, one is amazed that in the nineteenth century architecture and engineering were kept at a distance from each other and that the latter, where it was found to be necessary, employed the classical orders as if ashamed of its nakedness.

Adolf Loos always played a special role in the scene in Vienna. He did not join any group, and vehemently criticised the romantic air of the Viennese studios under Hoffman. How his battle against Ornament should be understood is evident in his own work. He had a passion for panelling the walls with precious materials. He also used hollow piers and non-supporting beams when, in his terms, this was required by the composition of the room. Some of his interiors were decorated with classical friezes in plaster: the Doric columns which emphasise the main entrance of the Goldman commercial building at Michaelerplatz in Vienna are mere 'decorations' (to be naughty). To accomplish this architecture, long spanning concrete beams were inserted storey by storey which, in the photographs of the carcasse, gave the impression of being suitable for oblong window bands. Far from it! They were filled in with bricks and, after plastering, a simple perforated facade appeared. This Viennese 'naughtiness' is not easy to tolerate. Very often Loos took up contradictory themes which he then pieced together like collages. Different facades in one building are often joined together as if they have nothing to do with each other. The interior composition of spaces, according to his 'Raumplan' (room-plan) concept, is interlocked and diversified, and surprising in terms of

their different heights. One of his projects, the administration building of the Herald Tribune in Chicago, is one of the strangest and most misleading statements in recent architectural history, not only because of its gesture, but because of its anticipation of many representations in contemporary art and architecture. Loos was a biting critic of the International Style, and I can only understand his entry for the Herald Tribune competition as a grandiose affront against modernism à la Gropius, Hilberseimer, et al.

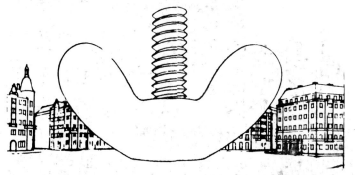

Claes Oldenburg, 'The Big Screw'. Design for a monument on Karlaplan, Stockholm, 1966

I think that if this building had been realised, idea and reality would not have agreed with each other. This building, in among all the

Hans Hollein, Vienna 1963: 'Transformation', a technical object becomes a cultural statement

Karlskirche, Vienna, by J.B. Fischer von Erlach, 1716—23

First Court Theatre, Dresden, by G. Semper, 1838—41

Wittgenstein's House, Vienna, designed by himself down to the last detail

other kitsch, would have looked monstrous and ridiculous. Steinberg's drawings picture similar American situations. Considering the appearance of the Herald Tribune Building, one might associate this gigantic Doric column with the wonders of the Antique world. But this is not possible if one reflects on its meaning. An office tower among many others in an American city with millions of inhabitants would soon have lost its spirituality.

Vienna, benefiting from her topographical situation, has always been a place where cultural controversies have been fought out. Here, the south German Baroque celebrated its splendid alliance with foreign styles in the masterly collage of the Karlskirche by Fischer von Erlach. Hildebrandt was by no means an orthodox classicist. His Upper Belvedere for Prince Eugen is a marvellous architectural achievement. It is a building which is not deep in plan, yet its clear geometrical facade and carved decoration gives the impression of a gigantic complex when viewed from the city. The enormous solemnity of the buildings on the Ringstrasse is still experienced with pleasure, although as cultural achievements they cannot compete with the unique musical creations of Beethoven, Schubert or Brahms, creations which have not been surpassed anywhere in the world.

Gottfried Semper, who was commissioned to design the Burgtheatre, left Vienna head over heels after only three years. He could not cope with the intrigues and the manoeuvres of the Viennese partner Hasenauer with whom he had to work, and who bestowed Semper's plans with an effusive local hue. So the Burgtheater, with the exception of the stage-set depot, as one of his late works has little in common with the strict discipline of his buildings in Zurich and Dresden.

In the twentieth century the music of Berg. Schönberg and Webern has gained an international reputation. The very few modern buildings in Vienna have not reached the same level. Like Neo-Classicism at the beginning of the nineteenth century, the clear, rational Modern Movement was only half-heartedly supported in Vienna. Only in the romantic expressionism of the Viennese 'Gemeinde' (community) buildings of the Twenties and Thirties has a generation of architects found its identity. This tendency, which was partially rooted in the school of Otto Wagner, gained spontaneous public acknowledgement because many details employed were known by the population as classical motifs.

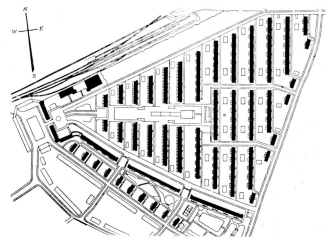

Plan of the 'Bad Durrenberg' quarter, Berlin, by A. Klein, 1930

Architects who adhered to the Bauhaus ideology certainly made fun of the playfulness of their Viennese colleagues. The latter were branded as secret traditionalists, and for that reason they were not appreciated for a long time. These 'Hof-Siedlungen' (courtyard estates) have a particular spatial quality, especially in terms of urban design when compared to the schematic linear housing estates; as for example the Dammer-stock estate in Karlsruhe by Walter Gropius or Onkel-Toms-Hütte and Siemensstadt in Berlin. (This subject has

Burgtheater, Vienna, by G. Semper and C. Hasenauer, 1874—88

Former stage-set depot, Vienna, by G. Semper, c 1875

'Karl Seitz-Hof', Vienna, by F. and H. Gessner, 1926

been dealt with at length in my book *Urban Space*, and therefore I can do better than to repeat myself, but concentrate my thoughts on the architecture of the buildings themselves.) I hope nobody minds that Vienna, at present my adopted home city, is always the focus of my reflections. In a similar way in which I teach my students to learn exemplarily from this city, my observations of architectural events receive their orientatioin from this background.

Heinrich Tessenow, despite his lectureship at the Akademie für Angewandte Kunst (Academy of Applied Art) which lasted for five years, never became an 'echter Wiener' (real Viennese). But because of his very honest, restrained architectural language, he certainly had some followers among the architects of council estates not only in Vienna. One aspect, however, should be pointed out in Tessenow's work. Shortly after the turn-of-the-century, at a time when many architects were still concerned with heroic design themes of the nineteenth century Tessenow concentrated all his efforts on workers' housing. In Rome, Tony Garnier was designing his 'Cité Industrielle' at the same time. The beauty and freshness of these drawings were never reached in Garnier's actual buildings. Both Tessenow's and Garnier's projects can be compared here as being representative for future generations.

In every cultural era there are two camps, the one of the traditionalists and the other of the avant-gardists. The two are mostly standard bearers of the same age and educational background but with different attachments to cultural heritage; the one cautiously weighing tradition, the other boldly questioning tradition. Attitudes can change with the life of an artist. However, at the time of competing for bread and recognition, not the most polite comments are exchanged. These, however, will be knowingly smiled at thirty, forty years later ...

One 'reactionary', the other 'progressive' ...

Can art be the one or the other? After a short time ideological hostilities disappear and what is left can be put in simple words: he was proficient, but incapable.

Art lives solely on the quality of meaning and the embodiment of it. All *ad hoc* publicity should therefore be handled cautiously, at least until superficial effects have died down. Even in times where culture is imposed by dictators, the so-called reactionary and opportunistic pieces of art will only reveal their true artistic quality and become recognisable for everybody after the ideological aspects have become meaningless. The artist is at liberty to freely choose his means of expression. He only disqualifies himself through sloppiness and incapability in terms of skill and design. Cezanne has created a fantastic œuvre with his innocuous landscapes and portraits; the Cubists with their violins, bottles and cuttings; Morandi with his arrangements of vessels etc. And none of them asked permission of the public to do this or that. Sometimes the price for the artist's freedom in his choice of theme and way of expression is lifelong isolation and a concomitant undervaluation of the artistic quality of his work. The artist's biggest enemy is the arrogance of the 'cultured' public. It only appreciates what is established and familiar. If one asks for personal judgement where no common interpretation exists, then a spiteful criticism breaks out condemning everything that is not understood. This has always been the case, and this touchstone of every new artistic generation is at the same time its challenge.

In this sense my criticism of the contemporary architectural scene should not be understood simply as being bitter about failed successes. They help me to clarify my point, to strengthen my position even at the risk of judging unfairly. Recently I was accused of working beyond the 'Zeitgeist' (spirit of the age). Indeed, for years this is what I have been doing with all my strength and devotion. My congratulations to the critic who has understood this. However, to be precise, I have always thought that I was working beyond contemporary needs, and that this was the reason why my

Gymnasium (Dalcroze Institute), Hellerau, 1910

Housing estate near Schwechat by H. Tessenow

Drawing from *Cité Industrielle* by T. Garnier, 1904

Drawings from *Cité Industrielle* by T. Garnier, 1904

Abattoir de la Mouche, Lyon, by T. Garnier, 1909—13

Maison Cassandre, Versailles, by A. Perret, 1926

architecture was not in demand. That it was all to do with prescribing a 'Zeitgeist' never came into my mind. The 'Zeitgeist' is solely created by artists and not by the public. It is a very natural thing that the older generation has to cope with their achievements being questioned, and therefore we do not mind their struggling against us. We for our part will not be supersensitive either, but nevertheless ask for a fair battle. Despite all hindrances, better arguments and achievements always receive the merit they deserve.

To re-capitulate the aim of this essay, I would like to mention that my extensive words have only the purpose of putting my criticism on a solid basis. I am not concerned about the normal change of generations, but that the arts worldwide are being made bankrupt. To posit and prove this has required this long prologue. However, the dispute between 'reactionaries' and 'avant-gardists' has another aspect; the former, building on a safe repertoire, benefit from immediate success; the latter, seeking new ways, are existentially threatened. Today, as the 'Moderne' in all its banality is enjoying cultural acknowledgement, everybody who tries to avoid this cul-de-sac by way of thorough studies of history is branded as a reactionary. Now it is he who is called to bear the pioneer's standard and to suffer the privations of a renewer. In both camps, only the best talents will survive the hardest test, while struggling for the realisation fo their ideas.

Tony Garnier, who won the Prix de Rome in 1899, renounced the traditional Beaux-Arts programme and devoted himself to a theme neglected in the nineteenth century: the industrial city. His architectural concepts are of ingenious clarity and void of any decorative romanticism. If one looks at Garnier's design for the Prix de Rome in the Beaux-Arts publications, one will notice that it is still fully in line with the bourgeois fashion-architecture of the fin de siècle. All the more astonishing is his reversal afterwards, which had very much to do with his sojourn in Rome. His projects are disciplined by an almost antique attitude. He was using the qualities of reinforced concrete, still new and revolutionary at the time, and refined this new material by way of an aesthetic design which respected its inherent constructional rules and logical composition. *Une cité industrielle* is a book which belongs to the most beautiful theoretical contributions of this century. Garnier had a strong influence on the 'Moderne' which was developing in the Twenties. But personally he rejected the idea of becoming a promoter of this scene. His buildings, however, did not fulfil the expectations of his powerful early work. Unfortunately he ended up in a structuralism, à la Perret, which was popular in France. Yet his Olympic Stadium and his abattoir of La Mouche remain outstanding achievements. Thus an avant-gardist became a bourgeois traditionalist. It was similar with Perret. Perret's early work contrasts in the same way with his later buildings in Le Havre. Unlike Garnier, Tessenow developed from being a poetic traditionalist into a classicist of the Thirties.

This pre-Second World War scene, so colourful and rich as it was, was abruptly ended in the middle of the Thirties when, on the Continent, dictators assumed political power. The official architectural canon for public buildings in German cities prescribed a primitive and inflated Neo-Classicism which had nothing to do with the delicacy and elegance of the era of Schinkel, Weinbrenner or Klenze. Buildings in rural areas were to represent the 'Heimatstil' (homeland style). Only industrial building was spared regimentation and could realise clear modern construction without problems. The debate on the architectural history of the Third Reich is immensely burdened, despite the fact that it is an issue of the past. The new rulers quickly realised that neither the aesthetics nor the technology of Modern Architecture were suitable to serve as the pretence of the Party. The same applied to Modern Art with its critical social aspects. The sober building bodies were anything but popular, their building technologies not fully developed, and therefore not reliable enough. To impress the masses, the Nazis fell back upon the

Albert Speer's studio, Obersalzberg, 1936

Factory in Westphalia by F. Schupp and M. Kremmer

approved monumental orders which, given the pressure of time they were under, could still be mastered in terms of craftsmanship. There was no time for new developments, and they did not want to run any risk. The model for a late Neo-Classical monumental architecture was found in the USA, and in colonial cities. Here, not only public buildings but also banks, office buildings and business premises were all alike in terms of the style described above. That the Nazis used the best materials and craftsmanship for the few pompous edifices they were able to build, can hardly be criticised. They sought to disguise the brutality of their regime with an appropriate (in their terms) architecture. In the history of urban design, the plans for Berlin are of 'excessive grandeur'. The urban geography would, however, have benefited from them. If one examines the different stages of planning, it appears that the initial proposals were much more differentiated and sympathetic to the urban structure in terms of scale. Only later did they become coarse in texture and lost in terms of space. A gigantic domed building of Boullée-like dimension was to establish the high point in this Berlin apotheosis. Sometimes one is tempted to think to oneself: 'They should have built all this stuff instead of making a war.' But this would probably have meant that the fascists would have been in power for an even longer period of time. In the Eastern Block this kind of idiotic despotism is perpetuated. The Stalinallee which could well have sprung from Speer's Bebauungsplan (development plan)

by means of an oppressive architecture, became the symbol for the rise of a young, communist state which did not want to be one. Later on, as soon as the images of socialism were fading away, the feeble architectural theory of capitalism came back into favour. If today the Berlin Wall was pulled down, the difference between the two Germanies would only be economic. Otherwise East and West do not contradict each other on the level of general cultural taste. The East simply did not succeed in finding an architectural language for its kind of society. It was not possible because its social order is that of a police state.

I was very shocked to find the Wall being dealt with as an architectural monument in an architectural journal published in East Berlin. We do not care for this kind of macabre joke.

A schizophrenia drug seems to exist in modern states, the effect of which is very unpleasant and painful. That a majority of the world allows itself to be placed under schizophrenic tyranny can only be explained by an analysis of power mechanisms which have got out of the hands of society. Or are there indeed pleasant sensations about self-destruction?

Or are there any natural automata which, in case of surfeit, order self-destruction?

Literature, music and art anticipated the apocalyse of the Forties long before it happened. I fear that the state of architecture, this mute imagery, has to be understood as a warning of an imminent

Domed Hall planned for Berlin by A. Speer, 1938

Karl-Marx-Allee (formerly Stalinallee), East Berlin, by Paulick, Henselmann, Hopp, Leucht, Souradny and Hartmann, 1951—57

No 6, Sandwirtgasse, Vienna, c 1860

No 42, Linke Wienzeile, Vienna, by Kmunke and Kohl, 1896—97

spiritual abyss. The last time that this abyss opened up was after mankind had inflicted the biggest self-destruction in its existence. I remember the boom of the bombers very well. But today they would sound like light music in comparison with the vast amount of destructive material available now. How can beauty ever grow on such a brutal background?

Architectural culture is interconnected but divided into two parts: the wide basis of common functional buildings for dwelling and working, and rising from that, the small apex of buildings which accommodate special functions for society. It is legitimate to design the latter in distinct manner, in order that they differ from functional buildings.

During the nineteenth century when the bourgeoisie was getting rich, it embellished its residential premises with all the attributes which were used by the dethroned aristocracy to stand out from the masses. The architectural language got so confused that it became necessary to find another way of distinguishing public buildings from private ones. The former, therefore, were isolated from adjacent buildings and set into a square, a park or sited on the top of a hill. But this step soon found its followers. In the Twenties the free-standing object as such became desirable for better living, working and resting in general. Only one aspect was not taken into consideration; given that everybody had the same rights, this demand would have meant the death of the city. Today this no longer needs to be proved. Modern cities are the built evidence. The majority of Americans claim that they do not want to have anything else other than the modern 'anti-city'; that only some 'fanatics' would still prefer New York, Boston or San Francisco. Let us wait and see what happens if, because of a new energy crisis, legs have to be used for walking again. Maybe then Americans will remember the good old European city again!

The confusion in architectural language became even more profound after the Second World War. As historical architectural features had been abused so much, architects thought that they had been left without any good examples and therefore attempted to express the special significance of a building by way of employing novel methods of construction. For the last thirty years the whole range of exotic structures has been tried out, for example, on churches. Flicking through publications dealing with this subject, one shudders at so much kitsch. In terms also of ground-plan design, anything conceivable has been put to the test. The underground church at Lourdes, or the one by Nervi beside Saint Peter's, can at best be called well-structured garages. These buildings have nothing to do with churches. Many modern churches can be mistaken for being industrial halls; some of them are deliberately designed that way to supposedly reduce the distance between the church and the faithful. To undermine the sacred in this way, given the significance of churches in the history of architecture, is for me the worst aspect of our present cultural decline.

Temples and churches have been acknowledged and valued at all times, even by unbelievers, as the most noble symbolic buildings. They received the best of artistic and artisan achievement. They exemplified the architectural tradition of an epoch. After the antique, they also became the most magnificent interior public spaces. Are there any other functions available now to compensate for the loss of religious feeling? The reading rooms in public libraries, the resting rooms in swimming pools or sport centres, station halls, concert halls or theatres? None of these functions can ever reach the mystic and symbolic significance of a place of worship. Every human being is touched by the enigma of life and death. The fateful and inscrutable dimensions of existence and non-existence are as overwhelming as they are frightening. Nature, in its monumentality and beauty, being the background for everything that happens, only cautiously reveals its secrets. To soothe his fears and to calm his senses, man has erected symbolic places on earth for the spiritual interpretation of

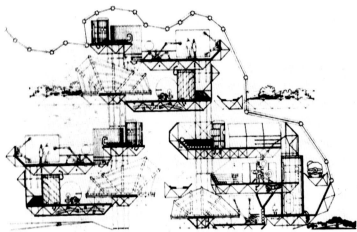
Design by Archigram, London, 1960s

his being. These buildings served as places of mediation between him and the unnameable enigmas; the addressee in this fictitious dialogue: a glorified human being, a God; the building: an idealised accommodation for the supernatural. I do not know whether this subject is definitely lost in architecture. For the time being, I am satisfied with the sacral buildings which history has passed on to us. We can live with these for another while longer. If an idea cannot be celebrated genuinely anymore, what else can one do but stick to things one is good at? In this consumer world people are not very interested in spiritual values.

At the beginning of the Fifties, the confusion about forms gave a fresh impetus to the development of new structures. Technology was less loaded a term than form, and immune from ideology. After a short period of time, the attitude spread that once the constructional requirements had been met, one had done justice to architecture. In a similar one-sided way, efforts were also concentrated on the solution of functional problems and cost-effective construction processes.

But despite the miseries of the post-war period, there are of course examples of an 'architectural' attitude towards design, and nowadays some buildings from that time gain sympathy despite their clumsiness.

One phenomenon, however, hit the devastated middle Europe quite unexpectedly: an exploding economic prosperity and in connection with that, an unrestrained building boom. In order to encourage building activities, governments offered special finance and depreciation schemes which could easily be abused. It is maybe only too natural that in this competition between 'more money' and 'more architecture', the Muse was the loser.

It is a long time ago that a person who commissioned a building demanded the best skills of architects and craftsmen, because his building was to demonstrate his honourable position in society. Also, the house of the poor and the house of the rich were easily comparable in terms of elegance, despite the difference in expenditure and embellishment.

The idea of making a lot of money in a short period of time has destroyed the quality of a building as such. Even the majority of buildings that do not need to meet high architectural demands have lost the elegance which I have mentioned above. That is also due to the fact that because of quick industrialisation, the building crafts have been ruined.

Responsible for all this are first and foremost the architects and planners who, burdened by growing competition, sell their souls and professional credit with the empty phrase: 'If I don't do it, another colleague will'. Can this fatal lack of self-respect still be overcome? Who is the first one whose eyes must be opened, the one who buys or the one who produces? Both are cheated at the moment.

The client who relies on cheap technology will soon have to pay for its defectiveness. He will also be bored quite quickly with superficial architectural cosmetics. The architect has tricked himself out of the most elementary professional fulfillment; and I cannot imagine that the easy money he earns can make up for the shame of blunt opportunism.

There are no less talented architects today than in the past. But now, to a much greater extent, they are condemned to inactivity or their creativity is just not asked for. Very often they take refuge either in the arts scene where it is still possible to get fair acknowledgement, or they lecture at schools of architecture which guarantee artistic freedom and survival.

But without practical challenge every theory is meaningless. I would very much like to prove my arguments with my own work instead of letting others do this for me. But to build under today's conditions is a damned humiliating business, not very sympathetic to the fulfillment of theoretical and artistic ambitions.

Illustrations in this article are either from the archives of *Architectural Design*, Academy Editions, and Rob Krier, or from the following sources: *Acte U. Moderne Kunst*, Berlin; Archigram Group, London; Paolo Faroce, *Piazza d'Italia*, Bramante Editrice; Johann Kräftner (photographer); Heinrich Kulka, *Adolf Loos*, Löcker-Verlag; Bernhard Leitner, *The Architecture of Ludwig Wittgenstein*, New York, 1976; César Martinell, *Gaudí*, Editorial Blume, Barcelona; *Propylaën Kunstgeschichte*, Band 11, *Die Kunst des 19 Jahrhundert*, Propylaën-Verlag, Berlin; Herbert Ricken, *Der Architekt, Geschichte eines Berufes*, Henschelverlag; Albert Speer, *Architektur*, Propylaën, Berlin; Steinberg's *Paperback*, Rowohlt; Walter-Muller-Wulkow, *Architektur der Zwanzigerjahre in Deutschland*, Langewiesche Konigssein; *Weltgeschichte des Architekture*, Belser/Electra; *Wiener Fassaden des 19 Jahrhunderts*, Böhlau-Verlag, Wien, 1976.

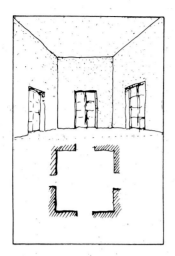 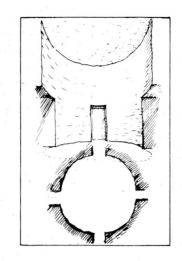 

# ELEMENTS OF
# ARCHITECTURE
Rob Krier

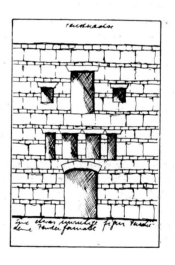

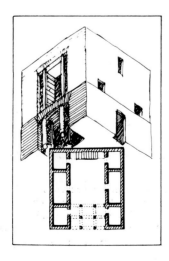 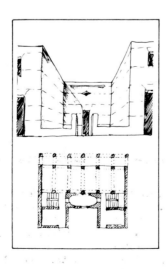 

# Explanations Relating to the

# Typology of Interior Spaces

The diagram shows in the horizontal the geometrical ground-plan forms: square, triangle, circle and the amorphous figure; and in the vertical the possibilities of transformation of these basic elements by way of addition, penetration, buckling, breaking, accentuation of the perspective, or effect of depth and distortion. These operations are put together side by side without any valuation. The examples presented here, however, are only a fraction of the variants created so far by human ingenuity.

At this point I would like to suggest that, from the history of building, one should picture the great variety of forms for oneself and refresh it again and again by way of drawing exercises.

## Addition

Addition is the most elementary principle of order. With the most simple way of addition, the elements are only closely joined and form an accumulation or a group. Their relation to each other ensues from the proximity, a so-called topological relation (Norberg-Schulz) resulting in an irregular, amorphous shape. In contrast to that, geometrical relation means a relation which is created by a geometrical principle of order, e.g. by axiality or parallelity. The basilica serves as an example in which several similar elements of space are arranged in parallel. In the perspective of depth, a series of impressions of closed spaces of nave and side-aisles emerges, whereas in the transverse direction, because of the transparency of the order of columns, the entire space can be perceived. By augmenting the heights of side-aisles towards the nave, the latter is especially accentuated and the orientation towards the altar is emphasised. We have here the different heights of spaces as a means of design to express the hierarchy of spatial elements.

## Penetration

1. Two or several spaces of different geometrical form overlap and merge into a new shape. In this process one space, or even both, will be deformed, i.e. their formal separation would be senseless, because it would yield fragments.

2. Two spaces being overlapped retain their independence, remain recognisable, and together create a new spatial quality. The crossing of the cathedral is a classical example: the longitudinal aisle and the transept penetrate each other and form a common space which is emphasised by a dome or a tower.

3. When two spaces overlap in a way that one includes the other, this gives rise to space within space. If the interior space is bordered by rows of columns and segregated from the enclosing space, the entire space remains to be experienced simultaneously. Classical examples of this kind of spatial penetration are to be found in Egyptian Baldachin Temples. The closer the two spaces move together, i.e. if they become nearly equal in size, one gets the impression of *one* space with a double enclosure. Louis Kahn, for example, sets circular spaces into square bounds for light penetration. Through different openings in the walls, the light is filtered when required, and indirectly led into the interior.

Further possibilities of transforming basic geometrical forms are the processes of buckling, bending, breaking, separation and fragmentation. This happens mostly if several elements of different geometrical shape should be joined together, and if one has to adjust to the other. Let us imagine an octagonal space which is surrounded by a corridor. Because of the given geometry of the octagon, it has to be buckled several times, in a sense to submit itself to the geometrical form. However, it can achieve an independent spatial quality if the buckling points, by expansion, are made into joints. Or another example, which very often can be found in housing construction in the nineteenth century, in Weinbrenner's work for instance: in a given

ground-plan form, which very often resulted from the shape of the site—perhaps a triangle as the residual site between two streets—the main spaces were inserted as independent forms—as circle, square or oval. Between them and the exterior skin, spaces of deformed shape remained, which sometimes had the awkward effect of being merely remnants, because they originated from something which was of more importance. So they offered the possibility of accommodating technical facilities. But often they are independent localities of the 'in between' and have enough spatial charm to accommodate staircases, for instance.

The 'perspective distortion', i.e. the artificial manipulation of the effect of depth, can be created by simple geometrical tricks, as Scamozzi did with his stage sets in the Teatro Olimpico in Vicenza; and Bernini in both his design for Saint Peter's Square, and his famous staircase in the Vatican, the Scala Regia.

The 'distortion' of a geometrical form can in most cases be attributed to fateful, historical events.

The examples of interior spaces listed here do not in any way represent a complete typology. The published drawings have emerged from exercises with my students carried out in the first year of their course. I am of the opinion that the decisions which form the design of a space, or a building, can only be completely understood if they have been apprehended through drawing them. It may be noted that my students draw exclusively in Vienna, so that they learn to recognize the city in which they study with all its qualities and the characteristic features of its local architectural tradition. That modern architecture thereby gets the shorter end of consideration is not surprising. The good examples in modern architecture are anyway too rare.

# Interior Spaces

As the starting point of architectural composition, the smallest spatial unity, the interior room, should firstly be studied. Normally an interior space has for its bounds: walls, piers, ceiling and floor, being the traditional elements. Windows and doors serve as connections with the exterior. By these, the technical elements of a space are determined. It becomes comprehensible and describable by the definition of its size, proportion (relationships between length, height

and width) and shape. These components refer directly to the function of the room because they allow for the residence of people, the accommodation of furniture and the execution of certain activities.

Shapes and atmospheres of spaces can be described. At first we recognize the geometry of a room, e.g. cube, cylinder or different forms mixed together. We can also specify the exact sizes and identify the proportions by relating length, width and height. Although we still describe rooms according to their basic geometrical forms, clear and simple spaces

nowadays have an almost elitist character. The so-called liberation of spaces by modern architecture has given rise to the unfortunate term 'flowing space'. Spaces were separated into areas, only able to function, but without contributing to better functioning. The repression of clear geometry has not resulted in a truly free and poetic solution of room forms, but in deformed structures, which no longer allow a meaningful relationship between wall and opening. The nature of a room is very much determined by its enclosure, which demarcates it from the exterior and turns it into an interior space. Let us consider the geometry: a sphere has a maximum enclosure. In geometrical terms, it cannot be connected to another form. In accordance with that, the circular room is not directional and rests in itself. Symmetry emphasises independence. In a rectangular space, the enclosure is created by the uninterrupted relationship between the four walls, especially the integrity of the corners. Rounded corners emphasise the enclosing character of the walls. By different treatment of the surfaces in terms of colour and texture, by arrangement of openings and incidences of light, the enclosure of a space can either be emphasised or broken.

More difficult is the description of the quality of a space. Very often when we describe their character, we talk about small, spacious, low, high, oppressive, friendly, comfortable, cold or warm rooms. Very often for these appraisals of a space, not only its geometry but also its attributes are crucial. In this sense every interior space offers a complete 'cultural image', given by proportion, light penetration, structure, furniture and accessories.

Already the accentuation of the surfaces confining the room adds to its character: dividing vertical and horizontal elements, floor texture, ornaments and mouldings on ceiling and walls, extensions, bays, colours and materials etc. The basic forms are equally changed by piers standing free in the room. New spaces 'within the space' are created. According to their purpose, they articulate and structure; they form transparent walls dividing the space, and because we move in the room, new perspectives, vistas and space relationships emerge again and again.

With the knowledge of these effects, the architect can give to a room the character which suits its function and significance. He can create a sacred space which makes people worship, a lecture-hall helping people to concentrate on listening, or an office room which, because of its functionalism, places work in the foreground.

Finally, owing to tradition, symbolic meanings can be attributed to certain forms. Archeologists and ethnologists have intensively concerned themselves with the significance of certain forms of space. Psychologists too, like C.G. Jung, made important contributions to the exploration of archetypes. Hanns Sieder, through extensive research in his book *Urformen der abendländischen Baukunst* (Archaic Forms in Western Architecture), comes to the following thesis: 'Considering ... existing forms, excluding each other in the circular or rectangular house, it is conceivable from what is known about the different stages in change of house construction in Italy and Greece, that we can trace back precisely the genesis of a rectangular house born out of a circular house via oval and apse-shaped preliminary forms. Decisions of that kind in favour of the circular or the rectangular house are rooted in the entire existence of the human being; they are not at all left to the free will. *Cultures not yet formed or no longer sound, make formless buildings.*' Sieder also maintains that certain geometrical forms of spaces gave expression to a corresponding physical and spiritual attitude: 'A non-directional circular space allows for relaxation and concentration. An oval-shaped space encloses two points of encounter. The form of the apse has risen from

the feuerschism ('firescreen') to the symbolic place of spiritual promulgation. A broad space becomes a place of preparation, a longitudinal space a route leading to somewhere. Both spatial directions meet in the square—the crossing—the place of ritually structured concentration.'

Of course the mythically influenced attitude concerning the effect of spaces does not apply to such a degree to contemporary architecture, e.g. housing construction. But it is crucial to bear in mind that certain rooms furnished in a certain

way can actually and significantly stimulate and influence the spirit and emotions of the inhabitants. This should also be understood as a warning to those who think that size and form of a room are only to be determined by the space requirements of standard furniture, and therefore forget about other spatial qualities. Only if we succeed in understanding the relationship between form, proportion, effect and usefulness can we achieve a meaningful and well-balanced composition.

KEY:
I   GEOMETRICAL GROUND FIGURES
II  ADDITION
III PENETRATION

IV  BUCKLING
V   SEGMENTATION
VI  PERSPECTIVE
VII DISTORTION

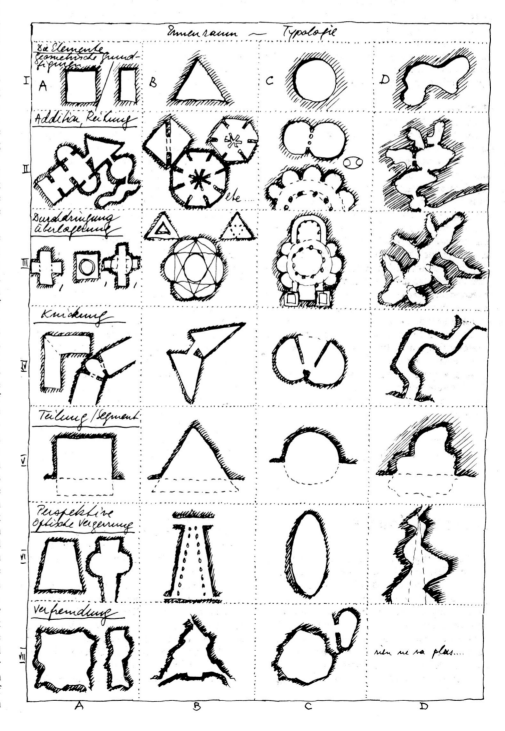

# Square Interior Spaces

The square remains clearly recognizable at best by means of an all-round symmetrical arrangement of openings. A well-balanced spatial effect without direction is shown in illustration 1, in which the openings are placed on the room axes. Going beyond this, the space can be structured by way of a subtle, square grid of pilasters, door lintels and beams. As the geometry of the space is specially supported, the square achieves an even more powerful expression (illustration 2). Also in illustration 3, we have a square ground-plan, but a space with a completely different centre of gravity because of the pier and cross-vault. Here, the tectonics of the vault are more important than the ground-plan.

In illustration 4 to 7, examples of structures are shown which—often for technical or functional reasons—in each case give to the space entirely different relations and directions. They alter the scale, and are confusing when it comes to describing the proportions. When divided by means of a row of piers (illustration 4), two equally relevant rectangular spaces are created. By the division of the square into three parts in one direction (illustration 5), the emphasis is laid on the 'main space' in the middle. This intensification can be reversed if the middle part which one enters is narrower than the two border areas. In this case the space in the middle gains the character of a route, and so the areas on each side become more significant. Illustration 6 shows an enclosed space with a skeletal canopy construction inside. A space within a space emerges. By that, the shape of the entire space is intensified; the canopy defines an almost sacred area and the edges become a silent zone; a threshold area which, although existing inside the space, does not fully belong to it.

The fully skeletal interior space (illustration 7) is of course only conceivable at a larger scale. Here one thinks of a space designed for special functions: the vast hypostyle hall of the Great Temple of Ammon in Karnak with its 134 sandstone columns; the base of the terrace in the Park Güell (Barcelona) by Gaudí; or the Danteum project by Terragni. Illustrations 8 and 9 show the centralisation of the square by way of rounded or bevelled edges. These 'manipulations of the edges', however, need to be minor in proportion to the sides, in order to avoid indistinct spaces. Otherwise this superimposition may easily provoke associations with a circular or octagonal space.

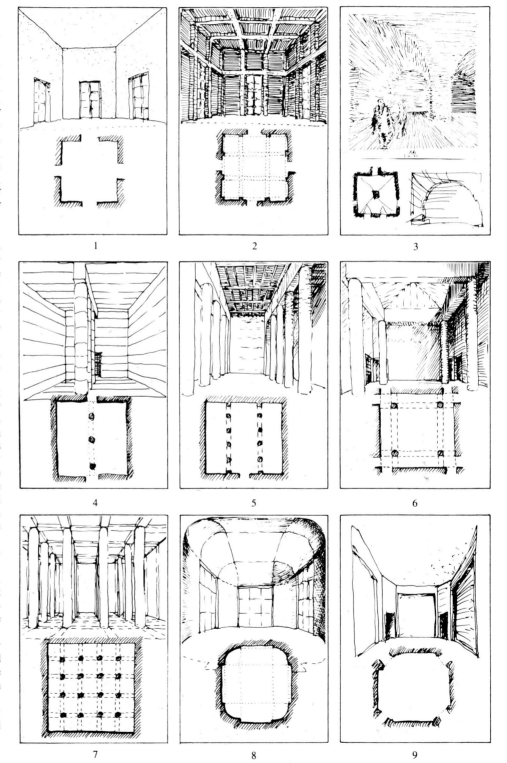

1

2

3

4

5

6

7

8

9

# Distorted, Basically Square, Geometries

Such spaces only possess the notion of 'centrality' found in the original basic geometrical form. Because of bays and frontal threshold areas, the following examples (illustration 1 to 3) have an intermediate position between 'pure spaces' and a series of spaces. Windows and doors in the bays form particular architectonic spaces with strong individuality. They almost force the middle of the space to remain void because the user's attention is focused on the bays.

# Rhythmic Series of Spaces
(illustrations 4 and 5)

Stations of a route with a small entrance area which functions as a 'border-crossing'. The anteroom has a clear orientation: a rectangle which accompanies the route and prepares us for the main space. This main space has the form of a square, but only at its final window front does the route end. The route is mainly recognizable by its series of spaces in perspective. Such an effect is prohibited in illustration 4 where four columns form an additional spatial filter, which psychologically 'stops' the route.

# Rectangular Interior Spaces

The simple, rectangular space with an open pitched roof (illustration 6) is an archetypal form for the house. It is to be found as sepulchre, as well as barn or garden house. This form of space is a good example of the significance of used materials. From the rush-hut to the solid stone shrine, the meaning and character of the space can thereby be subjected to a complete transformation. The surface texture determines the whole range of what is precious to what is merely make-shift. This is something that applies in general to every space, but here this fact is particularly evident.

In rectangular spaces (illustrations 7 and 9), the location of the openings is particularly significant. If they are positioned in the short sides (illustration 7), the room gains an airy atmosphere with a clear alignment along its longitudinal axis. By inserting rows of piers, this tendency is more manifest. The dark side-zones can be assigned to secondary purposes and activities. A longitudinal barrel (illustration 9) emphasises even more the closed cross-direction.

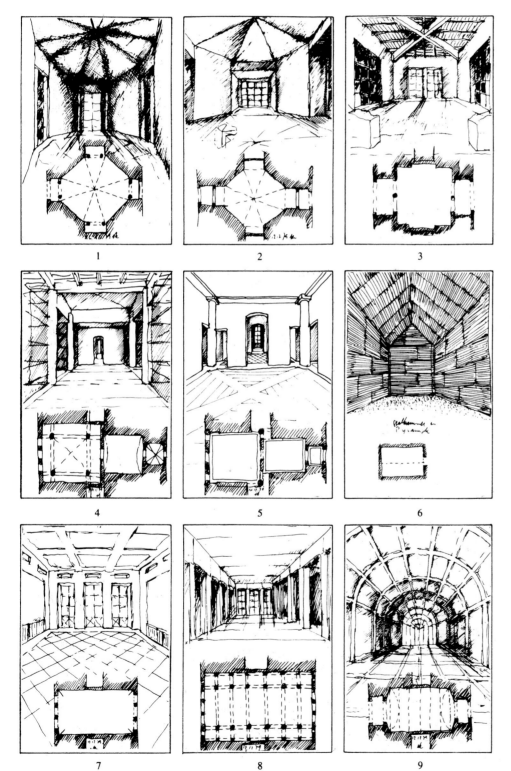

1

2

3

4

5

6

7

8

9

# Octagonal Interior Spaces

The variants of octagonal spaces presented here (illustrations 1 and 2) have, according to contemporary understanding, quite an exotic character. Nevertheless they do reveal some advantages. By way of stretching, octagonal spaces develop a clearly defined middle zone and two narrowing edge areas. The room thereby gains an intimate stability.

# Cross-shaped Interior Spaces

The crucial problem with cross-shaped interior spaces (illustrations 3 to 7) is the valuation of the two directions. Illustration 3 shows the interpenetration of two rectangular spaces of the same kind. If one focuses only on the inner part, the equivalence of the spatial areas is without any doubt still existent. But this space also has openings—doors or windows—which because of different valuations, immediately establish a hierarchy to the spatial areas. I would like in this context to cite Palladio's Villa Rotonda as an example, a building with a similar ground-plan where the effect of the different prospects is noticeable. A space having an intrinsic hierarchy of directions will be achieved, if for example the proportion of one part is changed. Illustration 4 shows the effect that can be gained by such an arrangement: one part of the space is elevated and thereby demotes the side parts to bays. A focus to the central space (illustrations 5 and 6) is reached by a cross-vault, or even more so, by elevating the crossing area. This space, which is called 'crossing' in centralised plan churches, has a supreme symbolic and mythical significance.

# Circular Spaces

Illustration 8 shows a round wall-shell within a square room, establishing a particular inner area. By the principle 'space within space' residual areas remain which have been developed to perfection, especially by the American architect Louis Kahn, with the result that interesting spatial effects were created. The circular space in illustration 9 belongs like square and cross to the

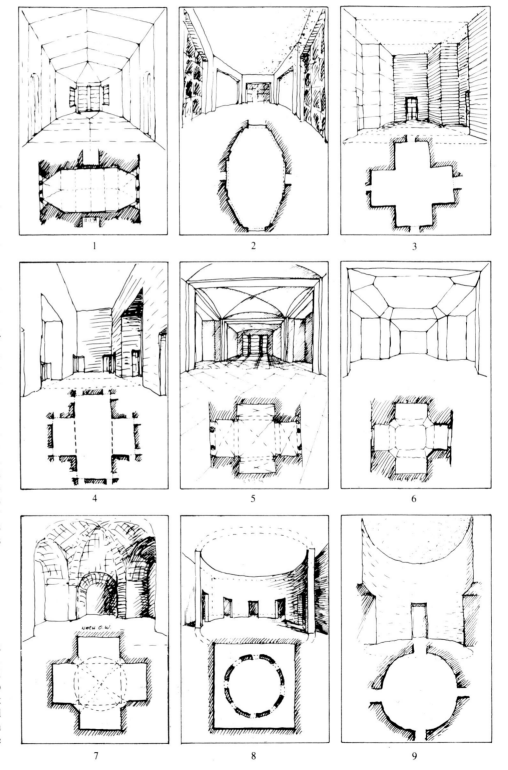

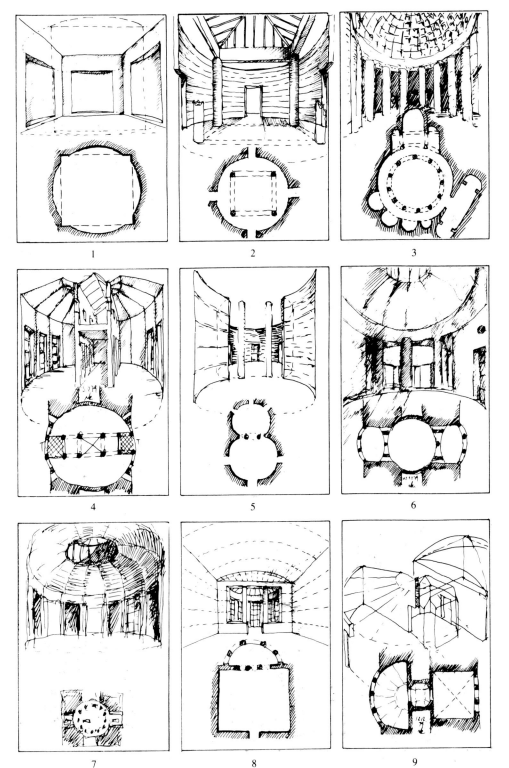

'archetypal forms' of architecture. The extreme spatial consequences require a well-considered discretion as to practical application. Psychological aspects have also to be taken into consideration; not every human being can cope permanently with such a powerful form.

The overlaying of two basic forms—the square and the circle—has been attempted in illustration 1. Compared to the altitude of the cube, the cyclinder is lower and therefore four segments remain as bays. This is an example of the differentiation of heights in a room and the resulting effects. Nowadays, thinking in three dimensions is very often neglected when it comes to design. The circular space with the square canopy in the middle (illustration 2) intensifies the significance of the central space. At the same time the room gives the impression of openness. A heterogeneous space with many side-rooms and bays (illustration 3) determines its centre by way of an inserted circular space formed by piers and covered by a dome. This is a technique which can also be applied to later adaptations of existing spaces where one often achieves valid architectural results. Circular spaces, to develop their spatiality and functional usefulness, need a certain minimum dimension which should not be underestimated. Especially height and form of the ceiling are crucial. In illustration 4 a high circular space is cut through by a bridge which, because of its transparent structure, allows perception of the overall space. This example also hints at the fact that circular rooms, being non-directional, are often used in a boundary position as the mediation of spaces with multidirectional structure. Illustration 5 describes two cyclinders which interlock. The transparent tangential zone offers a fascinating experience of space. A famous example in architectural history is the house of the Russian constructivist Constantin Melnikov. Illustrations 6 and 7 show circular spaces in each case being related to other rooms. The latter are designed as loggias or anterooms which surround the central space. These arrangements place on the circular space an ambivalent role. On the one hand, it is a space of tranquillity, void of furniture and other equipment. On the other hand, it serves as a kind of distributor, being in the best position to connect different routes and meanings. Illustration 9 actually belongs to the theme: composition of spaces. In plan, square, octagon and semi-circle form a rhythmic sequence of spaces. It is important to note how clearly geometrical forms can be brought into correlation.

# Addition and Penetration of Spaces in Practical Examples

The basic forms dealt with above can give rise to innumerable combinations of spaces; so it is out of the question that the employment of clear forms restricts creative imagination. Considering the mighty heritage of architectural history, the aberrations of modern architecture have proved one fact: spaces which can be described, which are conceivable in real terms, have the advantage of multifarious ways of utilization; still—and this fact cannot be pointed out often enough—a building exists in general longer than its initially assigned utilization. Illustration 1 shows a square, tent-shaped space, formed by an inner shell which separates it from a corridor. The route leads from a representational staircase—inserted in an ellipse—to an ante-space filter into the main room. In illustration 2 a directional rectangular space leads to a semi-circular one which has a relieving effect, promising a pleasant vista. Narrowness of the two spaces creates an important tension. In the space which is shown in illustration 3, it is the vaulting of the rectangular space which creates a relationship with the semi-circular forecourts. Illustrations 4 and 5 picture examples of simple series of spaces: through an entrance area one reaches a rectangular room which is terminated by a semi-circle which is its culmination. Illustrations 6 and 7 prove that it is also possible to give rectangular spaces a centre by way of widening and the superimposition of a central circular space. The last two examples, illustrations 8 and 9, deal with a rectangular space with curved ends. It gains different spatial effects by way of its inner configuration or widening.

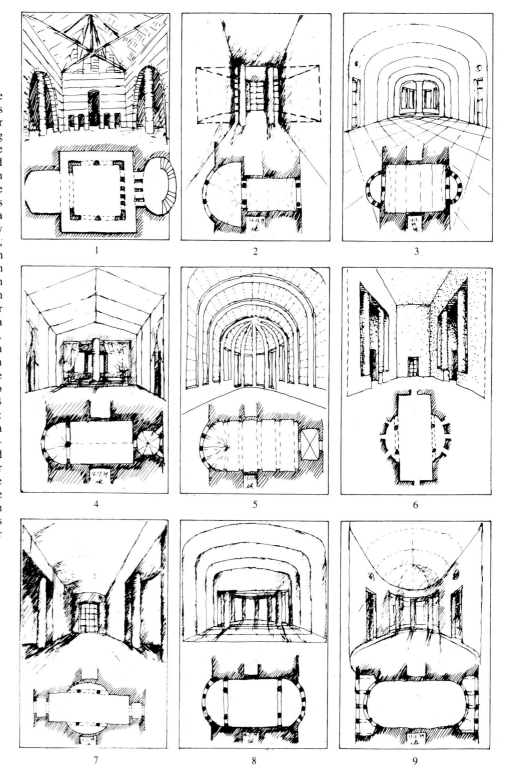

1

2

3

4

5

6

7

8

9

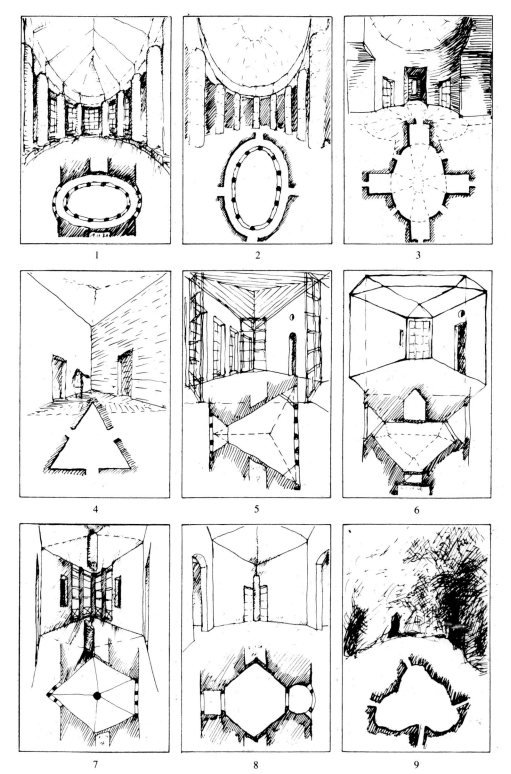

Oval-shaped spaces (illustrations 1 to 3) are not a modification of circular spaces, but stand as an independent type which, since the Renaissance, has always been seen as a contrast to the circle. The circle represents a mono-centric view of life, the oval shape a duo-centric one. The circle was favoured by the conservative, neo-classical theorists (Alberti, Bramante) in the Renaissance, whereas the moderns (Peruzzi, Serlio) preferred the oval, which reached its prime in the Baroque.* Of course from a formal point of view, the oval allows for similar operations as does the circle. However, similar to the rectangle, the oval is directional.

Triangular spaces (illustrations 4 to 6) are conceivable as special forms because of their pointed edges, which are difficult to fully utilize. For practical reasons, the triangle is often deformed; the edges are cut off or the three sides are rounded out. The Trinity churches of the Baroque are known examples of this. For secular purposes, the triangle is suitable as mediation of three distinct directions of traffic routes, or if a trunk road splits into two less important ones.

Special shapes (illustrations 7 to 9) stretch from all possible polygons to the irregularly modelled space—the cave.

To end this chronology, it may be remarked that all spaces should have in common defining borders. A space should always allow itself to be defined, described and understood without one having to take refuge in its atmospherical values to begin with.

* See Lotz, 'Die ovalen Kirchenräume des Cinquento', in *Römisches Jahrbuch für Kunstgeschichte*, 7th volume, 1955.

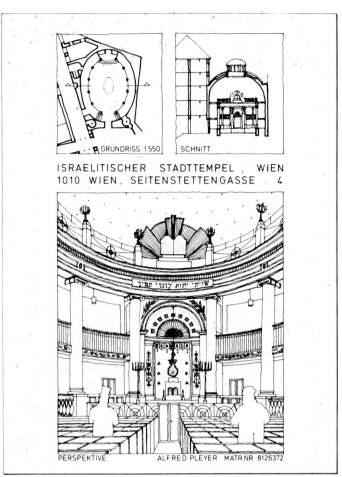

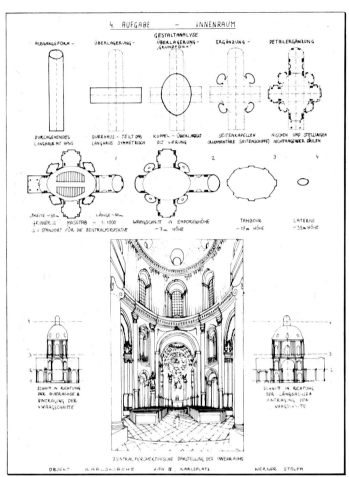

Student works on the theme of Interiors

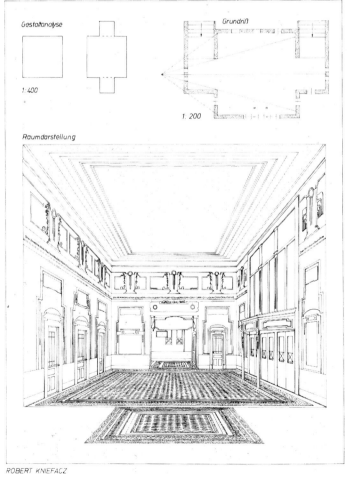

Hall of Columns, Parliament Building, Vienna, by T. von Hansen, 1873—83
(Ph: Bildarchiv d. Ost. Nationalbibliothek)

Court Library, Vienna, by J.B. Fischer von Erlach, 1721—35

Teatro Olimpico, Sabbioneta, by V. Scamozzi, 1588

'Knize' store, Vienna, by A. Loos, 1909—13

Diagrammatic interpretation of Palladio's ground-plans explaining spatial relationships

# The Art of Composing Spaces

Guided by the work of Palladio, I would like to demonstrate how spaces should be brought into sequence in order to create spatial and aesthetic relationships. It is not sufficient to be well acquainted with the quality of a single space as such. One must also be able to join spaces in a way that together they make an interesting composition.

### 1. Teatro Olimpico, Vicenza 1580

The auditorium deviates from the semi-circular Vitruvian type, common at that time, because of lack of space. It is a half amphitheatre in plan with rising tiers of seats. At the level of the top tier, the space is terminated by a colonnade consisting of blind and free-standing columns giving access to the stairs which are situated in the corners. This self-contained geometrical space appears as if inserted into an irregular larger one. The stage is linked with the audience by way of a rectilinear *scenae frons*: a richly structured facade with five openings through which seven 'streets' are visible in exaggerated perspective. This permanent setting, representing a city in Renaissance style, only allowed for the performance of classical plays.

### 2. Palazzo Porto, Vicenza 1549

The central space of this complex is an inner courtyard which is situated between two identical palace blocks, one for the use of the master and his household, and the other for guests. The two living areas with identical facades are situated between two public streets. One enters the palace through a vestibule with four columns supporting a cross-vault. From there a narrow corridor leads to central cortile which on each side has five axes. The space between the two columns in the centre is bigger than that between the others: 6,3/6,3/8/6,3/6,3 (feet). The columns are two storeys high and support a gallery on the level of the upper floor which is also held by smaller pilasters opposite the columns. The only element that has no symmetrical counterpart is the main staircase which is situated at one side of the courtyard equally distant from the two entrances. Palladio's intention was to focus attention on the cortile, being the most beautiful part of the palace. The staircase is rather modest in terms of spatiality. Palladio never created large-scale connecting spaces between the different floors.

1

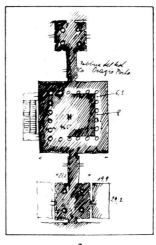

2

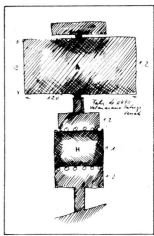

3

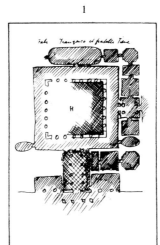

4

5

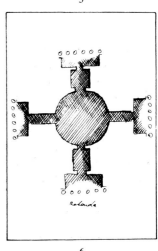

6

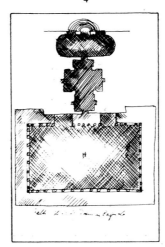

7

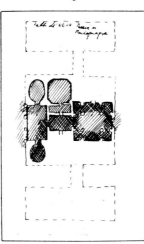

8

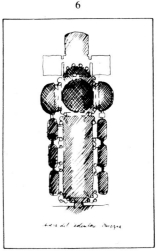

9

Ground-plans of projects by Palladio

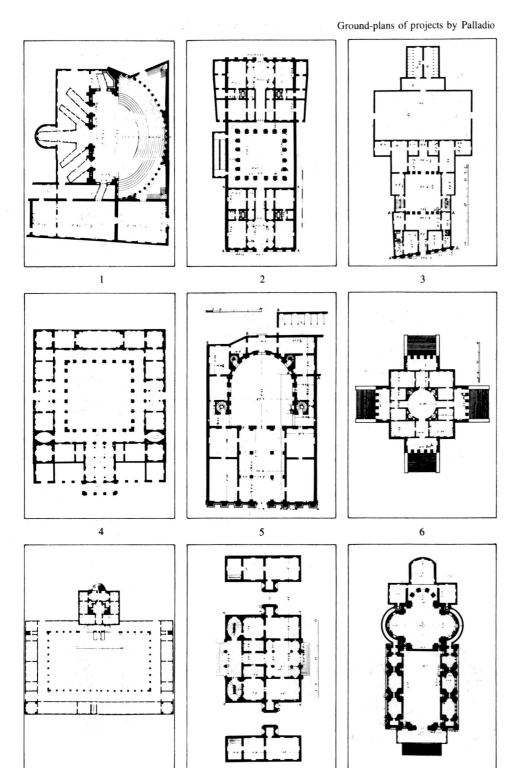

It was only in the Baroque that the staircase became a theatrical event. In the Venetian type of palace it always remained a secondary element. Much more important was the rhythm of spaces to be experienced when walking through the rooms: the vicissitude of wide and narrow, square and rectangular spaces suggesting either to linger or to continue one's way.

### 3. Palazzo Valmarana, Vicenza 1565

The sequence of spaces in this palace corresponds in a marvellous way to a cadence of different light intensity. One enters the building through a dark narrow corridor which leads to a dim arcaded hall, the transparency of which gives access to the bright square inner courtyard. The space between the columns diminishes from the middle towards the sides: 2/4/4/7/4/4/2 (feet). Therefore the light penetration is more intense in the middle of the space where one actually walks. On the other side of the courtyard one enters again a dim hall which mediates between the exterior and interior, and which on both sides is narrowed by one vertical axis. Then a dark corridor, which is shorter than the first one, leads into a garden which has a proportion of 2:1.

### 4. Palazzo Thiene, Vicenza 1542/46

The ground-plan of this palace is one of the most interesting in Palladio's early work. From a tripartite entrance hall, the portal of which is emphasised by a portico, one arrives in a square inner courtyard which is surrounded by an arcade. The corners seem to be denser because their high rectangular openings are only 4 feet wide whereas the normal openings are 8 feet wide. The same rhythm is applied to the organisation of the upper floor. Of interest is the variety of different spatial geometries which are arranged round the courtyard within the whole complex forming a consistent series of spaces. Square rooms alternate with oblong or transverse rectangular spaces. Corners are articulated by way of the octagonal room-width bays. The staircases are oval in plan.

### 5. Palazzo Porto, Piazza Castello, Vicenza 1571

Only two window axes have been built from this design (bottom right). The facade's dominant feature is a gigantic order of columns. A spacious tripartite entrance hall was meant to lead to a courtyard constituted by a rectangle and a semi-circle. The concave back wall absorbs movement in the direction of the longitudinal axis. Spiral staircases are grouped around the courtyard for access to the building.

### 6. Villa Rotonda, Vicenza 1566-67

The Villa Rotonda is the most consistent example of a symmetrical plan. The idea for such a composition was certainly also due to the topographical character of the site, a gently sloping hill. Palladio's intention, to constitute a relationship between the landscape and the building, is manifested by way of the broad external stairs on all four sides of the villa. As they rise towards the house, they form a built continuation of the natural hill. The entrances on all four sides are emphasised by porticoes for the enjoyment of the views all round. Inside, the two main axes run through narrow halls, slightly wider on the entry axis, and meet in a round central space which is two-storeys high and covered by a dome. In contrast to the plans which I have described before, it is not the axis of depth that is the main principle in this case, but the harmonious arrangement of rectangular rooms with a circular main space in the centre.

### 7. Villa Pisani, Bagnolo di Lonigo 1542

The main entrance is situated on a longitudinal side of the spacious rectangular courtyard which is mostly surrounded by an arcade. The columns of the arcade are interrupted in the entrance area giving way to a triple flight of stairs and a portico. The vestibule leads directly into the cross-shaped vaulted main space. The passage to the garden is through a transverse rectangular loggia which has two semi-circular terminations on the short sides.

### 8. Villa Pisani, Montagnana (Padua) 1552

From the street and an outside staircase, one arrives directly in the square main room which, by way of four free-standing columns supporting a transverse barrel vault, is divided into three zones. A corridor gives access to the loggia where the position of the columns corresponds to that of the main space. From here one has access either to the upper part of the building by way of two oval staircases on each short side of the loggia, or one continues on axis into the garden by way of an outside staircase.

### 9. Chiesa del Redentore, Venice 1576

The ground-plan consists of three spatial areas which correspond to different functions. The church is entered and a long rectangular nave provides the spatial frame for the processional route of the faithful. The direction of movement is emphasised by the longitudinal barrel vault and the double columns of both sides of the nave, which in each case constitute a niche. The nave terminates at the most important part of the church, the self-contained chancel which is covered by a dome and is accessible from all sides. The space is enlarged on three sides by way of apses. The back of the middle apse is a wall of columns through which the choir can be viewed.

### 10. Tempietto Barbaro, Maser 1580

A rectangular portico gives access to a circular domed space. To this space chancels are attached which are situated on the prolongation of the main axes. They have rounded back walls and thereby correspond to the form of the main space. The entire composition is orientated towards the centre, as with the Villa Rotonda.

### 11. Chiesa delle Zitella, Venice 1579

A rectangle, which is enclosed from the outside, includes a basically square main space in its central area covered by a dome. The edges of this room are bevelled in order to mediate square and circle. A rectangular anteroom supporting a barrel-shaped vault is extended in front of the main space. In contrast to the Tempietto Barbaro (10), the entrance axis is orientated towards a single chancel which is attached to the opposite side of the main space.

### 12. Chiesa di S. Lucia, Venice 1564

Here also, we have an enclosed, nearly square plan, which has no projections or additions. From an anteroom one arrives in a rectangular main space which is covered by a transverse barrel vault. The chancel is situated in the prolongation of the longitudinal axis with semi-circular niches added to it; it is flanked to the left and the right by minor square chapels with compound columns in the corners. The emphasised transverse direction of the main space creates a calming counter-balance to the movement axis of entrance to altar.

### 13. Palazzo Capra, Vicenza 1563-64

Similar to the Palazzo Porto (2), a rhythmical, symmetrical sequence of spaces develops along

Diagrammatic interpretation of Palladio's ground-plans explaining composition of spaces (continued)

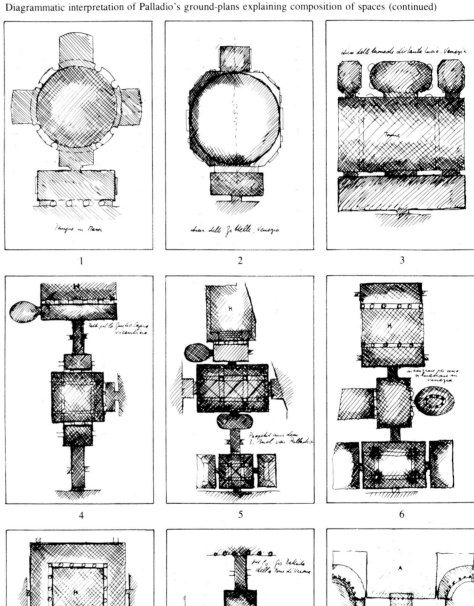

1

2

3

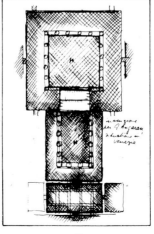

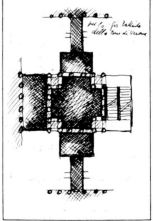

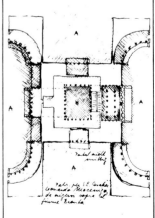

7

8

9

the axis of depth. A narrow corridor leads to a widened anteroom and finally to a quiet square inner courtyard surrounded by an arcade supported by four free-standing columns. Traversing the courtyard, the rooms gradually narrow again, leading into a loggia followed by a second and larger courtyard.

### 14. Project for a Palace in Venice 1553
This project discloses a very eventful sequence of spaces along a longitudinal axis. The square entrance hall is structured by way of four free-standing columns carrying a cross-vault above. This room is followed by two basically rectangular spaces at right angles to each other with similar dimensions which, when taken together, form a T-shape. The transverse room has semi-circular apses added to its short sides. From there one reaches the rectangular main room which picks up the motive of the four columns from the entrance hall. This space is enlarged to the left and right by a second axis. A small loggia creates the transition to the courtyard and, on the left, gives access to the oval staircase into the house.

### 15. Project for a Palace in Venice
When compared with the former example this project shows a similar organisation; however, the situation is different. The transverse rectangular entrance hall is bigger and again is constituted by four free-standing columns. A short narrow corridor leads to a smaller oblong hall which to the left receives light from the adjacent courtyard, and to the right gives access to the main staircase. A second short corridor leads through an arcaded hall into the courtyard which, on its opposite side, is confined by a second arcaded hall.

### 16. Palazzo Angarano, Vicenza 1564
The ground-plan is constituted by a sequence of three spatial units, where one prepares for the next. All areas have in common the motive of the position of columns but differently applied. The entrance hall is structured by way of two rows of columns in transverse direction and corresponding half columns recessed into the walls. The adjacent first courtyard, with an arcade, has the same width as the entrance hall, but is much deeper. The columns surround the courtyard only on three sides and, as arcades, support a gallery. The open fourth side of the entrance axis gives access to the main staircase so that the narrow passages on both sides of the staircase into the second arcaded courtyard appear as prolongations of arcades of the first courtyard. The larger courtyard is again surrounded by an arcade with the exception of the staircase area. By the spacing of the rows of columns, the width of the two other spaces is taken up again.

### 17. Palazzo Torre, Verona 1561
This building is free-standing and has an enclosed rectangular ground-plan. The two main intersecting axes determine the organisation of different spaces. The shorter entrance axis leads first of all into a rectangular space, then into the square main hall, and from there again into a rectangular space which accommodates the main staircase. The three rooms have the same width and are transparent because of the columns. The longer axis runs through the two side entrances which, by way of narrow corridors and small anterooms, leads again into the central hall. The principle here is the gradual widening of spaces towards the centre.

### 18. Villa Mocenico, 1564
The whole composition is orientated towards the central hall as is the case with the Villa Rotonda. The difference here is that a definite main axis exists. On two sides exterior spaces are created by way of quarter-circle arcades which prepare for the interior. Here we also have located the main entrances, whose porticoes consist of eight columns, whereas the side-entrances on the other sides only consist of six columns. One of the main entrances is especially emphasised by way of an entrance hall with free-standing columns and the adjacent main staircase.

*Ground-plans of projects by Palladio (continued)*

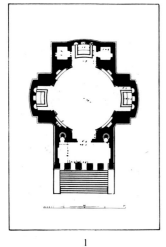

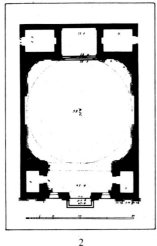

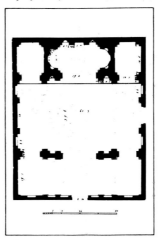

1

2

3

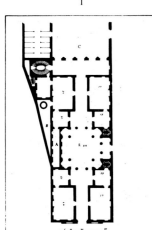

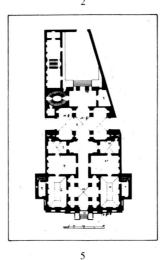

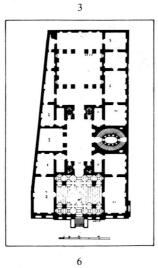

4

5

6

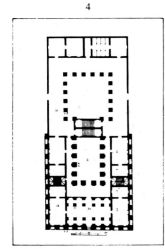

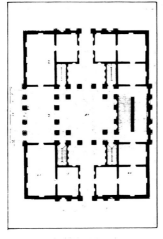

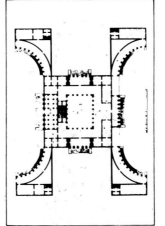

7

8

9

# Ceilings and Floors

These examples should only serve as a small indication of what we have lost in terms of treatment of the most important surfaces of an interior space—the floor and the ceiling. The surface of a room which we use each day, on which we walk all the time, cannot be dealt with only in terms of usefulness or ease of maintenance. The same applies to the ceiling, the termination of a space above our heads. A space's significance and use, independent from its size, can be adapted and structured by way of an intentional and painstaking treatment of these surfaces. Centralised spaces can be emphasised, lines of movements can be represented. No carpet covering the entire floor can have the effect which is so clearly achieved by separate beautiful rugs on a hard surface: the creation of small islands within a space, of informal borders which underline the employment and structure of the room; and which also, when looked at, give rise to a little happiness and relief. With one example, I would also like to explain the economic aspect of a sound treatment of surfaces. At the moment timber ceilings are very popular. But, many people prefer to use cheap veneered panels, or even foam rubber beams with an embossed wood pattern. After some years such junk becomes dusty, scratched and mean-looking, and has to be replaced by a new ceiling. Compared with this, we still find in old houses unpainted ceilings made of natural

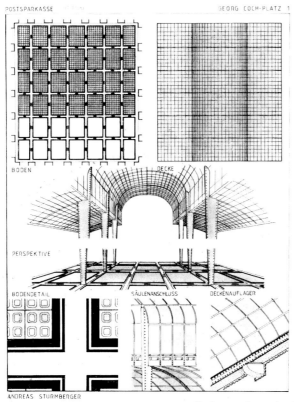

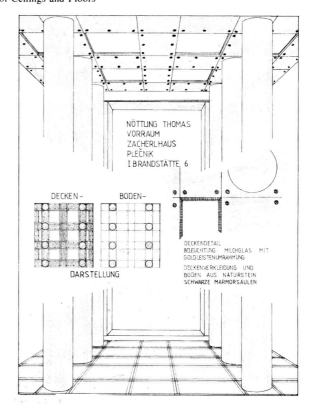

Student works on the theme of Ceilings and Floors

timber. Every few years they are cleaned with soap and brush and thereby develop over time a silky lustre, a patina, which makes the material, in the course of decades, more and more beautiful.

These three examples demonstrate the principle of floor and ceiling corresponding to each other. They show how the two surfaces are brought into into relationship by way of formal and constructional compositions. The first example (illustration 1) is the banking hall of Otto Wagner's Post Office Savings Bank in Vienna. The glass bricks of the floor correspond to the glass roof in its tendency towards dematerialisation. The piers emerge from the floor partitions and penetrate the roof into infinity. Also in the next example (illustration 2) the compartments of the vault correspond to those of the floor. The transverse arches of the ceiling are represented in the floor, the tiles of which repeat the diagonal principle. A classical, geometrical order is applied in illustration 3. Josef Plecnik created an almost sacral space when designing the entrance hall for the 'Zacherlhaus' in Vienna (illustration 4). From a shiny floor made of natural stone, black marble columns rise and break through an exquisitely detailed bright ceiling. The close positions of the marble columns, and their significance as part of the composition of the space as a whole, make it necessary to leave them without base and capital. What is most crucial is the envelope of the whole space.

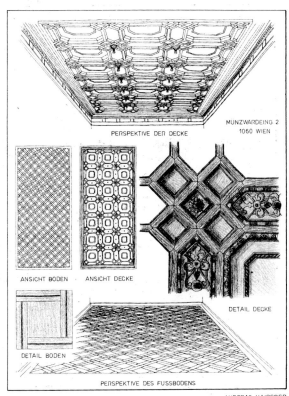

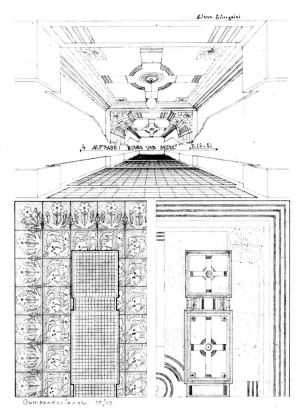

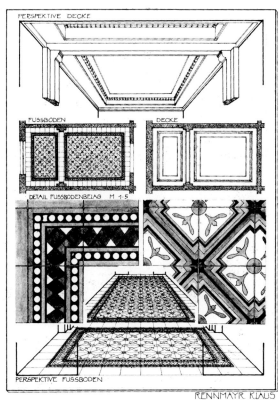

Roof truss of a hall for drying clothes, Burano, Veneto

Roof truss of the San Francesco church, Ravenna

Glyptothek, Munich, by L. von Klenze, 1816

Domed Hall in the Palais Rasumofsky, Vienna, by L. Montoyer, 1806—07

Floor of the Domed Hall, Palais Rasumofsky, by L. Montoyer, 1806—07

Court Library, Vienna, by J.B. Fischer von Erlach, 1721—25

Terracotta pavement under the arcades of the town hall area in Vienna, c 1900

Church am Steinhof, Vienna, by O. Wagner, 1905—07.

Student works on the theme of Columns and Piers

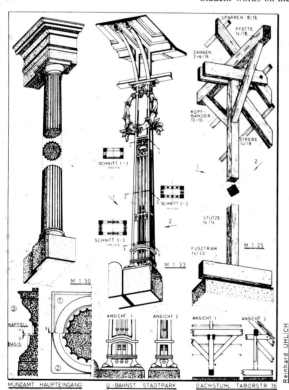

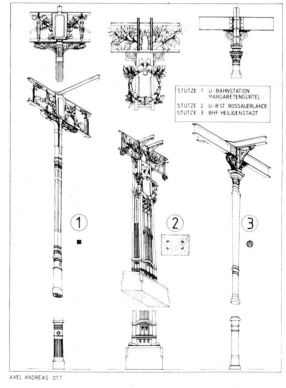

# Columns and Piers

Centuries of architectural culture have created an inexhaustible variety of forms of columns and piers. In Greek architecture epochs were named after their orders. Time and again the proportioning and decoration of a column or pier served as an indication and characterisation of a certain architectural style. The students' drawings which accompany this chapter should merely remind us of this. It remained for our times to give up the continuous refinement of this archaic form. A column has a relationship with the ground and has to carry a load; this alone should have been sufficient enough to bestow higher considerations on these two properties. Concrete or brick piers are problematic due to the vulnerability of their edges, which up to a certain height require special protection. The reason for the employment of banal concrete, steel or timber piers nowadays is very simple and clear: it is due to high wages which have far exceeded the price of materials. Experiments with concrete piers by Morandi or Nervi, for example, are no longer possible because the making of them has become too expensive. Exposed steel piers had to disappear from the classic repertoire of architecture due to rigorous fire regulations; and the quality of timber which is generally available today is so feeble that it hardly allows for artisan treatment. Does all this mean the end of the column and pier as an element in architectural creation? Of course, the high wages for fabrication are justified. But it would be important to make society appreciate the significance of architectural design and architectural themes, and to thereby gain public support which would make it meaningful again to learn from the Ancients how to use columns as a device of structure.

Arcade of a building from the Middle Ages, Bologna

Base of a pier in the Golden Hall of the castle Hohen-salzburg, c 1500

Base of a pier, Basilica San Vitale, Ravenna, 545

Four Piers of a stairwell, Vienna, early nineteenth century

Portal of the Heiliggeistkirche, Vienna, by J. Plečnik, 1910—11

Villa Sarregno, Santa Sofia di Pedemonte, by Palladio, 1569

# Doors

If one considers the conception of an interior space, every opening, whether door or window, means the violation of the wall. These violations, however, give the room its direction and its appropriate meaning. Doors play a decisive role in this context because they prepare the visitor for the spatial event to come. The significance of the door should therefore be considered from different standpoints.

A crucial pre-condition for our reflection is to recognize the door as being an important symbol. This banal statement makes sense if one examines the many versions of door formats available at present. We are used to a door having the form of an upright rectangle. Here the most popular sizes lie in the proportions 1:2 to 1:3 (illustration 1). Beyond this, the meaning of a door can vary according to its purpose. A low door for instance, which gives access to the parlour of an old farm house, clearly communicates that the private area is to be penetrated into. Doors of the same kind can be emphasised individually by way of additional openings on the sides or above (illustration 2). This kind of articulation also facilitates orientation. It is not always the scale of the human body which determines the size of a door. Especially in monumental buildings, the dimensions of the openings derive from the proportions of the receptive space. Quite often for everyday purposes, a door within a door was conceived, which could be used easily by people just wanting to go through. But when major events occurred, the entire over-dimensioned door was opened. Descendants of these palace doors are still to be found in bourgeois houses of the nineteenth century. The normal folding-door of a Viennese bourgeois house had a width of 1.25 metres and a height of 2.50 metres. But normally only one half was opened (about 60cm width)—seemingly nowadays a hardly bearable standard. (I am always amused to see some 200 students who came to my lectures at the Technical University in Vienna going in and out through such a narrow slit without anyone having the idea to open the second wing of the door; a good example of the relativity of function.)

More determined by function is the position of a door. But even under complicated functional constraints, it is possible in most cases to find an appropriate position which is in geometrical harmony with the room. Illustrations 3 to 6 show attempts to create a precise relation between wall and opening. Of prime importance are the pro-

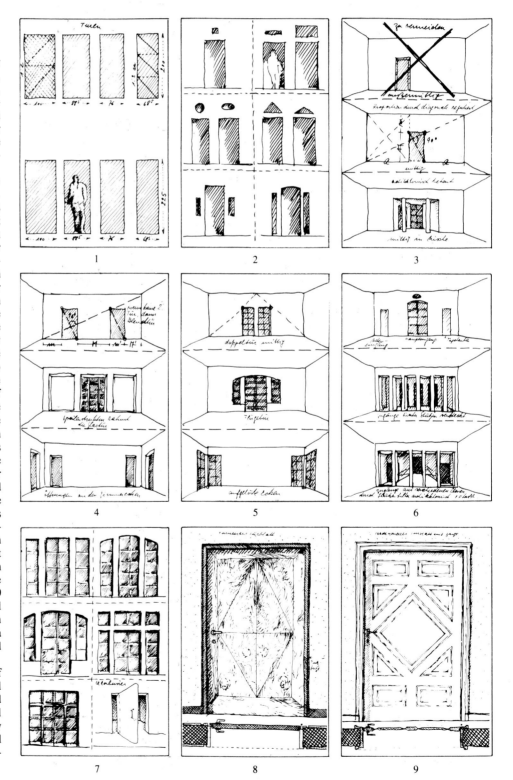

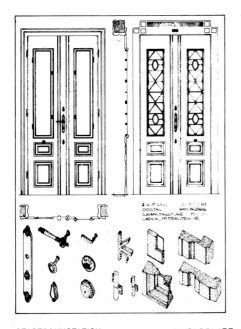

STADTBAHNSTATION      KARLSPLATZ

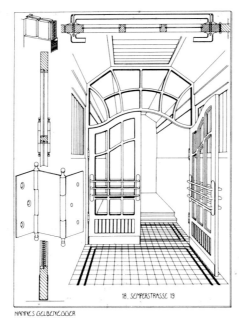

18. SEMPERSTRASSE 19

HANNES GELBENEGGER

TÜR U. TÜRBESCHLÄGE

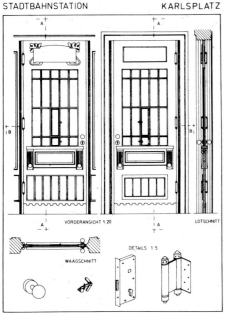

G. SIEGERT

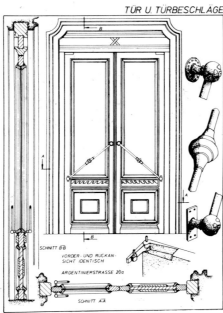

Georg JARITZ

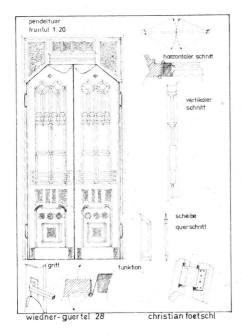

wiedner-guertel 28      christian foetschl

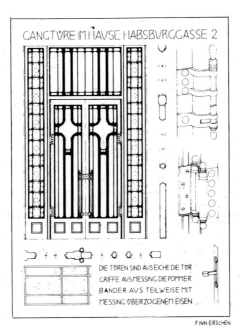

GANGTÜRE IM HAUSE HABSBURGGASSE 2

DIE TÜREN SIND AUS EICHE DIE TÜR
GRIFFE AUS MESSING DIE POMMER
BÄNDER AUS TEILWEISE MIT
MESSING ÜBERZOGENEM EISEN

FINN ERSCHEN

portions of door height and door lintel to the residual surfaces at the sides of the door opening. As a rule it might be appropriate to apply the system of proportion which determines the ground-plan and the elevation of a building also to the secondary elements such as windows and doors. If it is not possible to coordinate door and wall in this way, there are other devices to nevertheless achieve a harmonious space. Relatively simple is the creation of niches in a wall or the concentration of a group of doors and windows. A more difficult method, but one which helps to enrich the spatial atmosphere, is to insert bays which by way of piers are separated from the actual room and would cushion irregular positions of doors. This 'filter' in front of the opening would create a proper door space which is sympathetic to the functional structure of the actual room (illustration 6). The combination of door and window elements (illustration 7) is very appropriate, especially in the case of balconies, terraces and loggias. It is essential, however, that a distinction in terms of proportion and size between door and window is retained.

Before I end this section, I would like to mention some technical and constructional factors relating to doors. The violation of the wall caused by a door can best be overcome by fair-faced brickwork. The arrangement of lintel and door leaf is determined by the logic of the brickwork structure, and the frame is secured in the masonry accordingly. If the walls are plastered, the door frame in most cases simply surrounds the opening. And because of the incessant cracks between timber, plaster and wallpaper, the inhabitant realises very soon that these different materials are difficult to join properly. With old doors, these weak areas were resolved by way of richly profiled frames and the employment of beautiful timber. In addition to that, the decorators used mouldings to achieve a proper transition from door frame to wall. (A fantastic example is Otto Wagner's design for the management rooms in the Post Office Savings Bank in Vienna. The doors are treated as logical elements of the composition of the wall surfaces; the wall panels are therefore of the same timber as the door and window frames.) Our contemporary standard door sets offer few possibilities in terms of design. Today we can only concentrate on the quality of proportions, the material and colour. The steel frame is merely the representation of a frame around the plain door leaf. I think there is no longer any sign of the old type of door. Seemingly our building industry is only interested in crushing natural products such as timber into fibres only to later glue the stuff together again and to roll it into big sheets. The technique of making panels out of boards had led to astonishing results which became real works of art.

Student works on the theme of Doors

Former Stadtbahn station at Karlsplatz, Vienna, by O. Wagner, 1898—99

Palm House in the Burggarten, Vienna, by F. Ohmann, c 1900

House Knips, Vienna, by J. Hoffmann, 1923—24

Kinderschutzstation, Vienna, by J. Plećnik, 1907—08

The Secession Building, Vienna, by J.M. Olbrich, 1898

Zacherlhaus, Vienna, by J. Plećnik, 1903—05

Stadtbahn station at the Gürtel, Vienna, by O. Wagner, 1896—97

Building at Michaelerplatz, Vienna, by A. Loos, 1910

'Pawlatsche', popular Austrian expression for an arcade, nineteenth century

# Windows

The theme of this section is the window and its relationship to interior space. Its effect on the outside, the facade, is dealt with in the section dealing with the composition of the facade.

With respect to the relationship between window and interior space, first of all the window's function as the source of light is of great importance. To be more specific, we should talk about the effect penetrating light has on the interior space. To the same extent that a room is created by its wall surfaces, it is enlivened by light. One may think of a sunbeam striking upon a white wall or producing reflections somewhere in the room. The play of light and shade creating bright and dark zones in a room, motivates our awareness of the space—whereby not only the source of the light, the window, remains in our consciousness, but also the illuminated surfaces of the room: the texture of the walls, a sparkling floor, furniture or other objects which are given prominence by the light. Therefore the design of an interior space and the choice of materials and colours, should always take into account the effect of penetrating light.

One aspect that is quite often underestimated is the quality of light and its dependence on the time of the day, season, weather, cardinal points and intensity. All this results in certain though changing light atmospheres which we experience as harsh, soft, subdued, dazzling, sparkling, obscure, misty etc. It is also important to find out what quantity of light is appropriate for a space. Too little light can only be complemented by artificial illumination; too much or too direct light should be filtered with the help of devices such as shutters, blinds, lintels, transparent curtains and plants. Also forms of double skin wall construction which allow indirect (i.e. its intensity weakened) light to penetrate are a good and appropriate solution.

I do not allow my students to design horizontal ribbon windows, because I want them from the first moment on to tackle the problems of the window and its significance for the room. In the end, light coming from a ribbon window only has a very monotonous and banal effect on space. Therefore for housing developments, the appropriateness of ribbon windows is rather limited. I am of the opinion that single sources of light offer an opportunity for the space to be lit in a much more exciting way while they also allow the creation of areas in shade which are very pleasant in time of direct sunlight penetration. Equally doubtful in terms of benefit is the fully glazed wall or curtain wall. The excessive amount of light is exhausting for the eyes, and oddly enough, after having torn up the wall, one has to counteract the implications of excessive light by way of special sun protection equipment. The room itself is completely open only on one side, its geometry is destroyed, and the tension between inside and outside is diluted. But, if for functional or design reasons one wall of a room has to be left open, it is much better to apply an architecturally effective method, such as a row of piers or well-ordered bars, which would not destroy, but enrich, the interior space. As we are not in favour of the ribbon window, we have to come to terms with the position of the window. In general, we can establish that if a room is penetrated by light only from one side, which in the extreme case could be direct sunlight, an uncomfortable dazzle will easily result. But if the main source of light is balanced by a smaller window on another side—the opposite one would be best— or from above, then the room will be better lit. Even reflective masonry surrounding big windows can soften the contrast between the bright outside and the dark inside.

Not only is the way in which light affects the interior space significant when talking about the position of a window, but the view presented is important. The window frames a certain part of our environment and makes it into a kind of picture, but one which is changing constantly, very much in contrast to the motionless painting on the wall which can be an artistic substitution for what might be seen through a window. The awareness of the outside world is intensified by a cross window, or generally by windows with structuring bars, and becomes weaker the bigger the window opening is. Thus windows or glass walls which are too big, which open up the interior space totally, make the room uncomfortable; the feeling of safety and security is lost. If nevertheless a generous transition from the inside to the outside is desired, one should not think of achieving this in an abrupt way, but gradually, by way of loggias or transparent and lightweight projections (verandas for instance). If we consider all the points which are significant when dealing with the window—such as light penetration and its effect on the interior, light quality, position of the window, view from the window—then it becomes obvious that, strictly speaking, the window deserves as much care as does the actual room.

## Basic Forms and Bars

The square, the triangle and the circle are the basic geometrical forms for the window. The latter two, however, have to be regarded as special forms. Traditionally they were used for spaces of eminent or solemn significance. It is therefore recommendable to treat circular and triangular windows with great care, and to use them sparingly so that their meaning is not trivialised. Otherwise they would degenerate to negligible graphic attributes too quickly (illustration 1). The classic window has a rectangular upright format. For thousands of years of architecture, this kind of light source has proved to be the most economic both in terms of construction and in optimal terms of function. Related to constructional considerations, the simple argument against broad windows is that they violate the wall considerably. In terms of function, the upright window has evolved to meet most simply and efficiently the requirements for sufficient light, air and view.

The square window, although representing a precise form, is a very abstract, and, in addition, a very banal format. It can be appropriate if in the composition of a facade it is used as a harmonizing element together with other forms.

Stock Exchange, Vienna, by T. von Hansen, 1874—77

Former stage-set depot, Vienna, by G. Semper, 1873

Leopold wing of the Hofburg, Vienna, by P. Luchese, 1660—66

49

In anonymous rural and urban architecture, square window formats are almost exclusively used for secondary utility spaces. Very rarely are they applied to domestic buildings. Several times when I thought I had discovered a square window, it turned out in fact to be slightly rectangular. The exact square has also the disadvantage of appearing distorted when viewed from a certain angle; face to face it takes on a horizontal format. The most common window proportions result from the division of the circle into three parts (1:1.16); the division of the circle into four parts (1:1.4); the golden section; and the proportion 1:2.5 (illustration 2).

I should mention that all my recommendations concerning different aspects of design, although they may sound irrefutable, always allow for first-rate exceptions. I refer only to Le Corbusier's 'ribbon window' or Aldo Rossi's 'square window'. Window divisions are firstly related to the kind of opening one is dealing with. They have to comply with basic function, such as opening, ventilation and cleaning. In addition to these, window bars can be employed for the aesthetic structuring of the window plane (illustrations 3 to 8). This latter design responsibility has been very much neglected in the recent years. It was thought to be enough to satisfy the passion for an unhindered view by way of panorama glazing, which was made possible by the products of the glazing industry. Very often as a result, the intimacy of a space was destroyed; tasteless 'curtain culture' was the user's response. Because of all these reasons one should go back again to sensible divisions for the window and reconcile its design with that of the facade.

The simple divisions, depending on the kind of opening, are horizontal or vertical, and the superimposition of these two. The common 'window-cross' has been quite successful. It is economic in terms of timber consumption and handy in terms of ventilation and cleaning. One of the top casements can open separately by way of a lever mechanism. The lower side hung casements also allow for the unavoidable curtains to be moved aside when the window is to be opened. If people have fear of heights, they can lean on the closed casement and look out through the other opened one (illustration 6).

The examples in illustration 4, which show different arrangements of bars, are rather decorative. These windows are special in terms of their structure, their figuration, the tension between larger and smaller divisions; they have an independent architectural significance. The

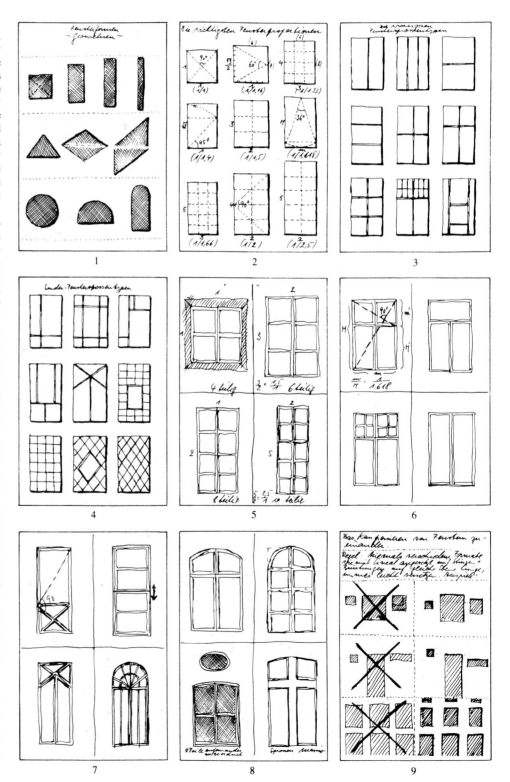

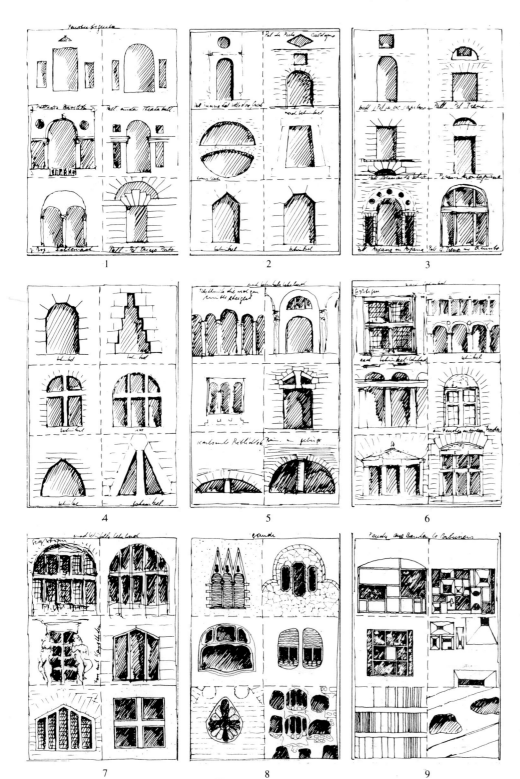

1

2

3

4

5

6

7

8

9

window surface itself becomes an important element of design. It would be precarious to replace these kinds of windows by synthetic or panorama glazing. They would destroy the texture of the facade.

A successful bar pattern in architectural history is the multiple division of the window in fairly exact square compartments (illustration 5). For this type, the different thickness of bars is a characteristic which results from the constructional functions of frame and thinner elements.

Vertical sash-windows, common in Great Britain, allow for the greatest graduation of ventilation. Both halves of the window can be moved upwards and downwards and they can remain in any position—air can come in either from the top or the bottom. Special forms of windows dealt with here are seen as derivations of the rectangular window (illustrations 7 and 8).

As regards the combination of different window formats, I would like to suggest a simple 'peasant's maxim' (illustration 9):

1. Different window formats should never line up with either their lintels or their sills. Otherwise this would be a typical result of T-shape thinking. Cut the formats out of dark cardboard and move them around on the facade drawing; you will learn quickly how to avoid banal solutions. The tension of the formats one to another is geometrically measureable.

2. One should be careful with the addition of identical formats both in the horizontal and the vertical direction. If one tries to alternate the sizes storey by storey, it will become evident how lively the relationship between opening and masonry can become (illustration 9).

**Window Figures**

Window figures are created when different formats are brought into aesthetic interdependence. They can even be set in an architectural frame and therefore become a particular element of the facade. I have sketched some examples to explain what I mean: Palladio (illustrations 1, 2 top, 3), Schinkel (illustrations 2 bottom, 4, 5 top and middle, 6, 7), Gaudí (illustration 8), and Le Corbusier (illustration 9).

Window figures are always divided into different elements. Openings with different functions and meanings are combined to form an 'image'. The result is an exciting conduct of light into the interior and an architectural articulation on the outside. Window figures are also especially addressed to exterior space. Here the relationship to the overall facade is crucial.

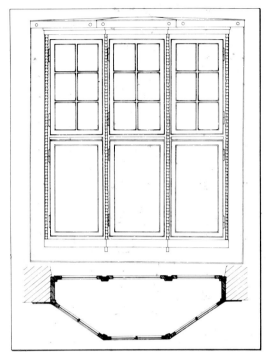

No 70, Sternwartestrasse, Vienna, by F. Federspiel

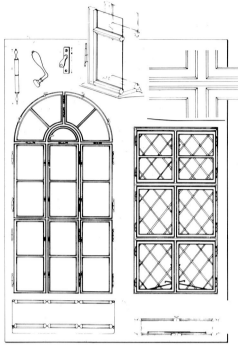

No 12, Akademiestrasse, Vienna, by C. Vostrovky,
and 'Schloss Schönbrunn', Vienna, by G. Aicher

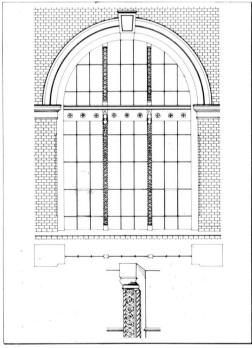

Markethall in Landstrasse, Vienna, by J. Dürrhammer

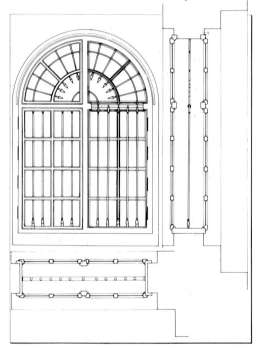

Building at Minoritenplatz, Vienna, by E. Aicher

## The Window as Room Divider

The examples in this plate have been measured up by students from old Viennese buildings. They show the refined treatment, the richness in detail and the significance which was applied to the window. The bay window in illustration 1 is designed as a special room. A window is not merely 'a hole in the wall', it defines a real space with an area in front of the window, a breast-wall zone and an exterior space. This is best described by the experience we have when approaching a window: we are no longer inside and not yet outside. Behind us lies the protecting room and in front of us the exterior world. The window has to be easy to reach to be used. It should also tell us something about the significance and situation of the rooms behind. Illustrations 1, 2 and 4 also show windows where the space between exterior and interior windows can be used. By this, an optimal response to different climatic needs is ensured, because several casements are available to be opened or left closed. This works much better than even the most sophisticated modern ventilation systems (if they work at all!). These hints advocate that the window should be understood as a spatial element and not as transparent wall.

A special theme is introduced by the arched window (illustrations 2, 3 and 4). Although dividing the arch is an extremely risky task in aesthetic terms, this was often undertaken to emphasise certain windows over others. In the nineteenth century the arched window was also used in engineer-designed buildings. But the bars in the arch already usher in the domination of the machine (illustration 3).

Heinrich Tessenow had strong opinions about filling in parts which came into conflict with the overall form; especially when—as with the arched window—a rectilinear division meets with an arch so that unsightly residual areas remain. As much as an arched window can be very attractive, these difficulties should not be brushed aside. Alberti has probably expressed the most severe restriction concerning this problem: 'In these Sorts of Apertures various designs have been commended; but the best Architects have never made Use of any but Squares and strait Lines.'*

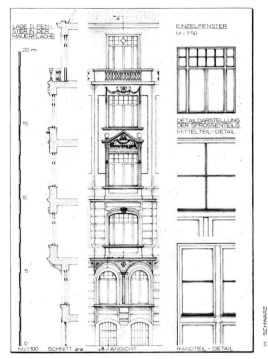

Student works on the theme of Windows

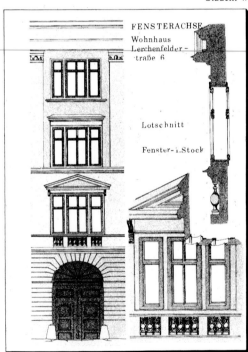

H.HALBRITTER

H. R. Schmidt

## Facade and Window Axis

Further reference to a contemporary grievance is given by these facade segments. The windows let us imagine the wonderfully high rooms behind. It is really questionable whether the lowered ceiling heights in council housing represent such striking progress. Of course they are cheaper than the old ones. Bathrooms and toilets are expensive; but would anybody think of ignoring them in council housing because of cost factors? I just want to hint at the priorities which should govern us when making buildings. Unfortunately one priority, the quality of the space, has been most easily renounced. And what also been lost in this context is the high, representative window. Therefore, again an admonition

from Alberti about the treatment of windows: '...from whatever side we take in the Light, we ought to make such an Opening for it, as may always give us a free Sight of the Sky, and the Top of that Opening ought never to be too low, because we are to see the Light with our Eyes, and not with our Heels; besides the Inconvenience, that if one Man gets between another and the Window, the Light is intercepted, and all the rest of the Room is darken'd, which never happens when the Light comes from above.'

Without intending to anticipate the section on facades, I would like to show here parts of facades which relate to the vertical graduation of windows. The examples demonstrate that in former times the valuation and meaning of

particular storeys was also applied to the design of their windows. The arrangement in these buildings represented social conditions, because different storeys were inhabited by members of different social classes. Nevertheless today we are attracted by this differentiation not only for nostalgic reasons. It allows for spontaneous orientation, the recognition of particular storeys and a precise architectural designation. To achieve this, it is not absolutely necessary to use different window formats for special storeys. Different materials on the facade can also support a similar effect.

* Leone Battista Alberti, *Ten Books on Architecture*, English translation published by Alec Tiranti, London 1965, chapter XII.

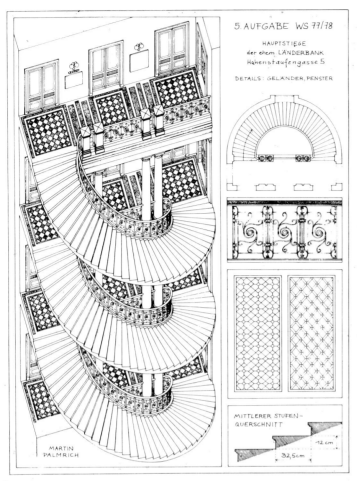

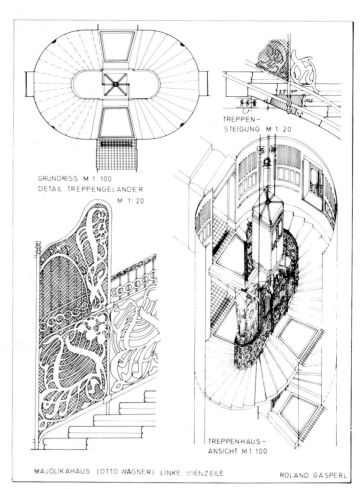

Student works on the theme of Staircases

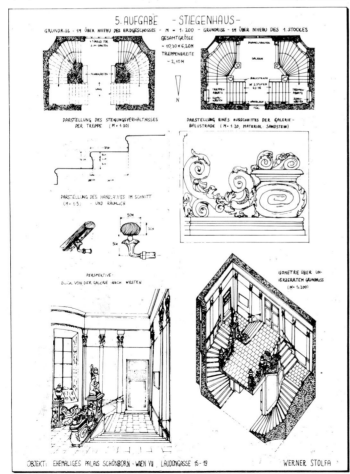

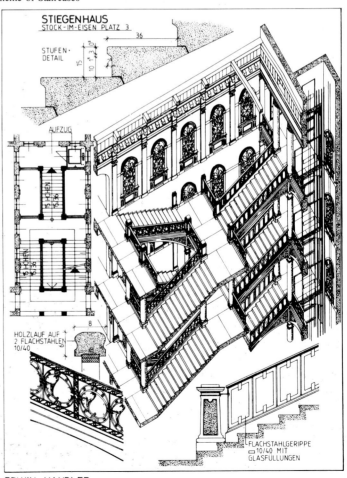

# Staircases

The staircase is the vertical element of access in a building, which enables one to ascend and descend from one storey to the next. The primitive forerunner of the staircase is the ladder. It is the shortest connection between two places, but it is also steep and hard to use. In most cases it is not firmly installed in order to be used flexibly, and therefore lacks any proper spatial or architectonic quality. The other extreme, the ramp, allows for an almost imperceptible transition from storey to storey. The differences in height are very easily overcome. But the space which is required for a ramp is considerably larger than for a staircase because of the gentle rise of the former.

The function of a staircase determines its form and at the same time shapes the enclosing space. We perceive either a straight flight or two opposite diagonal flights which cut through the space, or a winding movement which turns upwards. The way a staircase runs; whether it requires a—typically vertical—well; where it fits into the ground-plan; its construction and material are all aspects which contribute to its form.

A short glance at history shows the changing emphasis which was given to the staircase. The Romanesque spiral staircase, for instance, had no light and having the shape of a tube filled a special recess in the masonry or was pressed into a circular tower. It fulfilled the purpose of transporting people upstairs and downstairs like a vertical corridor. During the Gothic period, the outer skin of the staircase was articulated by arcades, columns and tracery. Light could therefore penetrate and it could be looked through. In the sixteenth century we have stair towers which were extended vertically beyond the buildings they belonged to, having a 'crow's-nest' on top. Here the motive of the staircase is linked with a social function. In Baroque palaces the well of the staircase becomes a representative Hall. The staircase itself is gorgeous in detail, oversized and runs up in several flights. It is full of light and sometimes ends under a mighty cupola. The actual purpose of the staircase is dominated by the notion of representation. The typical staircases in residential buildings in Vienna reached their prime in the nineteenth century: curved stairs of natural stone, free projection over one side, minimal thickness of material, generous gaps between flights, artistically designed banisters and profiled handrails. The well was in most cases illuminated by a rooflight and quite often, besides water-taps, contained sculpture or stone benches. In Otto Wagner's residential buildings these details have been executed as real masterpieces.

In the years after the war, space was cut down for economic reasons and the large-scale staircase has been sacrificed without hesitation. This is why we have merely functional staircases in our modern buildings. They appear as an addition of disjointed sections with tiny landings and minimal flights. The generous gap between flights, which allowed the view from storey to storey, has almost completely gone.

The staircase, which formerly was an important area of human communication, has to be given back its appropriate significance in a building. Solutions for stairs on a more appropriate scale are still possible. It is not difficult to create them as spaces which we find pleasant, which receive enough light and allow views to the outside, and which are enlivened by a sunbeam penetrating through a rooflight. The widths do not need to be enormous: 1.10 metres to 1.20 metres is enough, if landings intervene which allow for conversation or resting on a bench.

The most important requirement of a staircase is that the degree of rise is as gentle as possible, in order to reduce to a minimum the effort necessary for climbing. To determine a convenient angle of rise, first of all the stride of a human being must be taken into consideration, which on average has a length of 63 cm. It is assumed that the movement in vertical direction requires a double effort in comparison with the horizontal one. This means in arithmetical terms, one tread and twice the riser should make 63 cm. The most comfortable staircase according to Viennese tradition has risers which are 14 cm high and treads of 35 cm width. Unfortunately most staircases are steeper with risers of 18 to 19 cm because a reduction in floor space can be achieved. If the height of steps is less than 14 cm, the bottom line of convenience is reached because difference in altitude is only very slowly mastered.

The staircase and its surrounding space are an essential part of the architectonic composition of a building. Its function of giving access to different storeys can only be achieved in a meaningful way if this quality is immediately obvious; in other words, if it is clear that the staircase serves as a device of orientation in a building. Today one makes do with technical and graphical guiding systems instead of organising routes and stairs in a way that by their position, by way of their relations to the entrance and their particular form, the plan of the building can be understood and visitors can easily orientate themselves. If a building has to accommodate several staircases, the hierarchy of significance and frequency in terms of use can be manifested in design, while unmistakable areas are created. Form directly fulfills function. Here the whole richness of typological variations is at our disposal.

'Neue Hofburg', Heldenplatz, Vienna, by G. Semper, 1869

Official staircase in the Post Office Savings Bank, Vienna, by O. Wagner

Building at Michaelerplatz, Vienna, by A. Loos, 1910

**Staircase**

Similar to the ladder put against a wall, the straight stair is the simplest solution. Illustration 1 shows an example which is fitted into a frame of piers and beams. If a straight staircase is situated in a bigger space, access to the different storeys can be given by way of a gallery (illustration 2). This type works very well in public buildings. The respective stair to the next storey is easy to find, and the gallery allows all rooms on one level to be entered without difficulty. More economical in terms of space, and therefore better suited for housing developments, is the square well with straight flights of stairs of the same size as the landings (illustration 3). One common solution is the development of two straight flights with an intermediate landing (illustration 4). If the landing is bordered by an exterior wall it is possible to arrange for the well to get natural light. Three flights of stairs (illustrations 5 to 7) have to be seen primarily as being related to representation. They almost directly ask for 'dignified striding'. The example in illustration 5 is suitable for repetition over several storeys. A broad staircase starts with one flight until the intermediate landing is reached, at which point it turns into two flights which are narrower than the first one. However, the example in illustration 6, where two flights rise in different directions from the intermediate landing, has its best effect if applied only once in a building. In illustration 7 two flights of stairs from opposite directions meet to become one stair. This form is recommended especially for passage-ways with two entrances, as they can be approached equally from both directions. The type in illustration 8, which is a flight of two stairs with preliminary steps leading to it, demands integration into a high space which allows the whole staircase to be looked at from elsewhere. A very costly solution is shown in illustration 9, where stairs change their direction on every level to give access alternately to opposite sides. This can be suitable for special solutions.

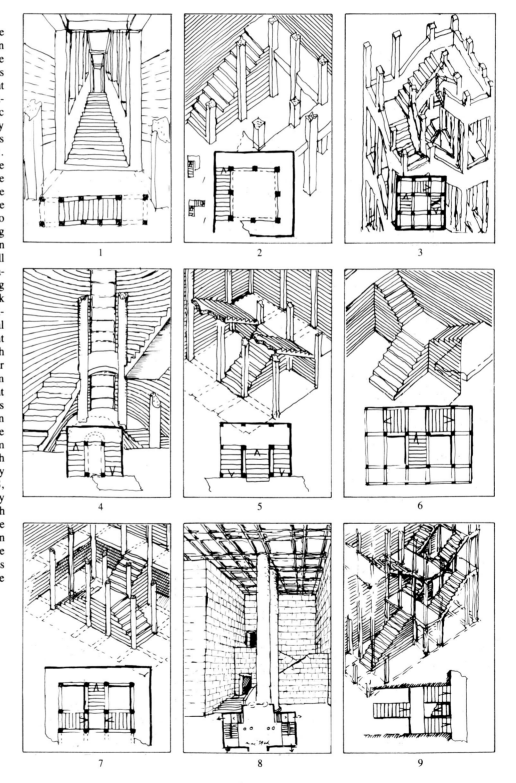

1

2

3

4

5

6

7

8

9

The geometrical modification of straight staircase leads to spiral stairs. In difficult spatial situations, for instance corners, a two-flight staircase on a triangular ground-plan can be applied (illustration 1). A variation of this form is a stair rising in three flights on the same ground-plan (illustration 2), but here only a small landing remains. Two flights of stairs on a polygonal ground-plan—for example a hexagon (illustration 3)—provide the well with a high spatial quality. Illustration 4 is more related to the exploitation of a geometrical form where the sides of an octagon are constituted alternately by flights and landings.

Illustrations 5 to 9 show examples of spiral staircases. The very narrow newel staircases (illustrations 5 and 6) are difficult for elderly people and unsuitable for bigger objects to be transported. This is not the case with winding staircases on half-circular (illustration 7) or oval ground-plans (illustrations 8 and 9). Here it is also possible to find one's own walking rhythm by either climbing on the inner or the outer side. What should be avoided is the alternation of circular and straight steps, because this makes it very difficult to find one's natural walking rhythm.

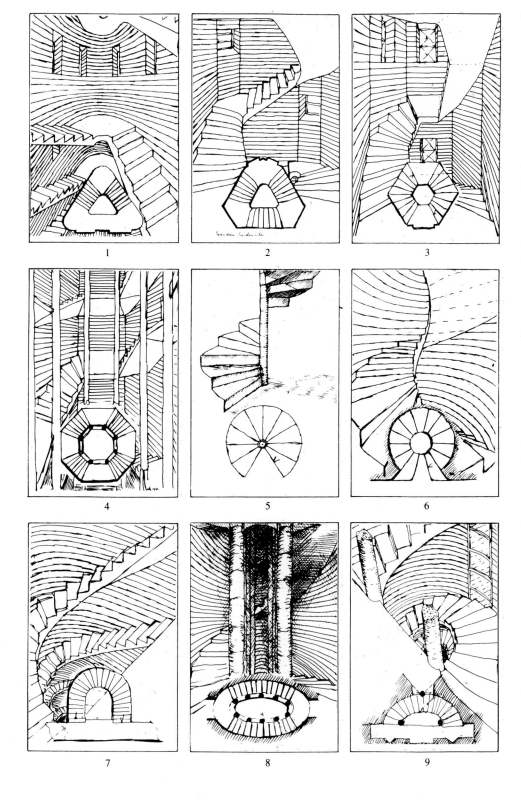

1  2  3

4  5  6

7  8  9

Staircase in a building from the Biedermeier period, Vienna, c 1830

Staircase in a building from the Biedermeier period, Margarethenstrasse, Vienna, c 1830

Spiral staircase, second building phase of the Post Office Savings Bank, Vienna, by O. Wagner with O. Schöntal, 1910—12

Staircase for the officials 'Beamtenstiege' in the Post Office Savings Bank, Vienna, by O. Wagner, 1910—1912

Staircase in the building No 1, Seilerstätte, Vienna, first half of the nineteenth century

Entrance hall of a residential building in Landstrasse, Vienna, by J. Brychta, 1862

Staircase in the monastery 'Klosterneuburg' near Vienna, by J. Kornhäusel, 1834—42

'Majolikahaus' at the Rechte Wienzeile, Vienna, by O. Wagner, 1898

# Facades

The facade is still the most essential architectural element capable of communicating the function and significance of a building. I say 'still', having in mind its theoretical destruction proclaimed in the twentieth century where the ideology of the free-standing object, visible from all sides, became predominant. The perfection of the building body had priority over the creation of a specific 'show-side' facing the street. It is only in recent years, after the rediscovery of the importance of the public realm and the value of urban life, that the facade regained a new valuation.

The facade never only fulfills the 'natural requirements' determined by the organisation of the rooms behind. It talks about the cultural situation at the time when the building was built; it reveals criteria of order and ordering, and gives an account of the possibilities and ingenuity of ornamentation and decoration. A facade also tells us about the inhabitants of a building, gives them a collective identity as a community, and ultimately is the representation of the latter in public.

The root of the word 'facade' stems from the Latin 'facies' which is synonymous with the words 'face' and 'appearance'. Therefore, if we talk about the 'face' of a building, the facade, we mean above all the front facing the street. In contrast to that, the back is assigned to semi-public or private exterior spaces. Both these phenomena of front and back relate—roughly speaking—on the one hand to public responsibility and on the other hand to the private self-representation of the inhabitants. Compared with the more representative character of the street facade, the back of a building is more open and communicates with courtyard, garden and landscape.

The often-used framed facade made of light material and glazing is too standard in type and too abstract in character for housing developments. It does not allow for aesthetic differentiation and is too vulnerable and transparent. Such a 'skin facade' has nothing to do with the appropriate facade for a residential building, which should be more closed and concealing towards the street, in order to protect the private sphere of the inhabitants. All these requirements are still best met by the solid facade whose massive, protecting exterior wall is perforated by openings to let air and light penetrate into the interior of the building. Also, in terms of energy consumption the solid facade is without doubt much more appropriate, because its exterior wall has a higher thermal storage capacity. In Austria, the energy problems caused by glass facades have already been taken into account. In public buildings a smaller proportion of windows in a facade surface is allowed as compared with previous years. This proportion between opening and plane has at least stopped the unhindered development of curtain walls, and has helped the solid facade to gain new topicality.

The composition of a facade, taking into account the functional requirements (windows, door openings, sun protection, roof area) is essentially to do with the creation of a harmonious entity by means of good proportions, vertical and horizontal structuring, materials, colour and decorative elements. Since Vitruvius architects have been trying to develop metrical relations which would give an ideal order and structure to the facade—and also to floor plans and rooms. This was thought to be the way of achieving absolute beauty. Especially in the Renaissance, such attempts were referred to systems of numbers and rules of proportions. Plato's philosophy was taken as a basis, as were the thoughts of Neo-Platonism. Saint Augustine approved—and so Renaissance artists were thoroughly convinced that the whole universe was a mathematical and harmonious creation. By such thinking, rules were established which Wittkower describes as follows: '...If the laws of harmonic numbers pervade everything from the celestial spheres to the most humble life on earth, then our very souls must conform to this harmony...' *

But the aim of reaching a harmonious beauty cannot be achieved only in this way. One needs only to consider that the oblique view given from the bottom of a building, together with the constantly changing contrasts and effects of depth caused by light and shade, prevent us from perceiving such truly calculated proportions exactly. Nevertheless it seems very important to me to examine window proportions with the help of the golden section, and equally to study the proportions of opening and parapet, base and total height etc. This exercise will lead after a while to a 'natural' sense of pleasant, harmonious proportions, e.g. a well-balanced composition. It is the rhythm in architecture which, similar to music, rouses emotions in us. Therefore it is possible to transfer conceptions of musical theory

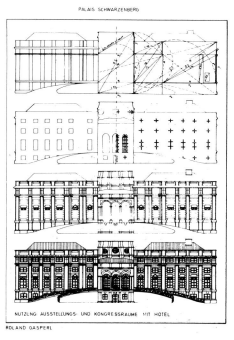

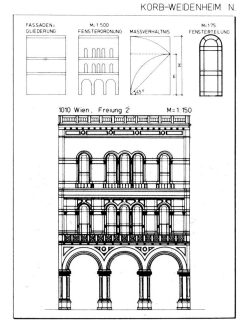

Student works on the theme of Facades

directly to architectural composition. The polarities of tension-relaxation, event-interval, accord-contrast; the principle of repetition; the process of the theme being carried through in variations; all create the rhythm of masses, planes and lines.

Let us, for example, reflect on window openings which repeat themselves again and again, which in succession with the wall elements, create the contrasts of open-closed, dark-light, smooth and rough surfaces. At the same time because of periodical repetition they produce a quiet order and vary the same theme from storey to storey by way of—for instance—rhythmical diminution towards the top (appropriate because the light quality increases).

An important aspect of structuring the facade is to make a distinction between the horizontal and the vertical elements, each of which can, in themselves, create an adequate general effect. Normally the proportions of the elements should correspond to those of the whole. Accordingly in low broad buildings, windows, bays, etc., broad proportions would predominate, whereas in high buildings slender elements give a sense of the large being found in the small and the small being found in the large, as it is similarly experienced in nature.

Following the ordering principles of a facade, the constructional conditions can be made visible, e.g. by channelling the bearing forces into piers. This articulation of verticality would emphasise a particular effect of the facade. However, this is not to put construction too much into the foreground or to show every nail or joint,

but to reveal the nature of construction and craftsmanship.

Besides construction there are many other things necessary in terms of function or simply narrative elements which add to the animation of the facade: window surroundings and lintels to articulate the independence of the windows, rain-pipes, shutters, roof projections which give shade, materials that emphasise the masses (rustication) or loosen them (reflecting marble), window boxes and Virginia creeper give the building a summer or winter appearance.

The horizontal layering of the facade results from the different areas of function. In principle, a facade should never be designed without horizontal differentiation. A clear differentiation is especially appropriate between the ground floor, the ordinary storeys and the attic. The facade as 'built border' acts in a similar way to the portal: in German the word for wall is 'Wand' which has to do with 'wenden' (to turn) or with 'Wandlung' (change); the wall is therefore the place where the exterior turns into the interior and vice versa. This transitional zone has the function of exchange, becoming more lively if the surface has a certain plasticity and if movement is evident. By way of wall projections, ledges and pilasters the plane of the surface develops three-dimensionality, becoming a relief, whereby light and shadow, foreground and background, become perceptible.

The facade as a whole is composed of single elements, the latter being entities themselves with an expressive capability of their own. The composition of a facade, however, consists of

structuring on the one hand and ordering on the other. The elements base, window, roof etc., which by their nature are different things, will also therefore be different in their forms, colours and materials. All these parts should remain recognisable individually, although the common language binding them to the whole has also to be found. However, not every means of connecting or matching is sensible: for instance to locate the upper edges of windows and doors in one line would contradict the different meanings they have. If the heights are staggered, the common factor could relate to similar proportions or shading gradations of a basic colour.

If we do not approach the design of a facade as an autonomous work of art, but in context with adjacent historical facades, it is necessary to employ different elements which separate the new from the old as well as ones which join and connect both. Thus the choice of elements should first of all be related to the language of the historical facades. Parts of them, or particular aspects, will be taken across, a purporting continuity being achieved by such a thematic approach. But genuine continuity is only conceivable once the independent quality of the new facade, and its new conditions and demands are upheld. The relationship between old and new is in any case a dialogue, a conversation between the past and the present.

*Rudolf Wittkower, *Architectural Principles in the Age of Humanism*, Academy Editions, London 1973, p 27.

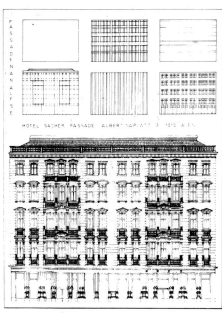

WALTER LEXMÜLLER

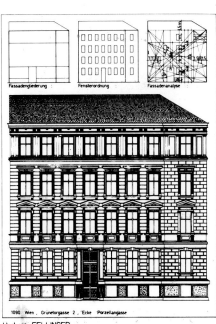

Herbert FELLINGER

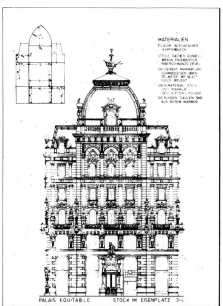

G. GRIGAR

This plate shows fundamental possibilities for the design of a facade. First of all, with small sketches, I would like to again hint at the decisive role geometrical proportions play for the harmonious appearance of the facade (illustration 1). Considerations of this kind are, of course, not to be separated from the whole building body. If, because of a disadvantageous site or restrictive building regulations, an unsatisfactory solution of the facade will transpire, this can be at least partially prevented by careful composition, i.e. a deliberate zoning of the facade (illustration 2). Yet when applying this kind of deliberate zoning, harmonious geometrical proportions have to be paid attention to (illustration 3). By the distribution of windows in the facade, a particular effect can be emphasised or suspended (illustration 4). Here the possibilities range from a regular distribution of equal windows to an irregular and figurative arrangement. Windows can be combined in small groups to form particular figures, or they can divide the facade by being almost separate elements (illustrations 5 and 6).

While windows are the most important means of composition, the facade itself can be treated as a sculptural part of the building. Specific parts of the building can be exposed (illustrated 7), whereby the foreground and the background of the facade are determined (illustration 8). The superimposition of different building parts is yet another subject of composition, which will be dealt with again in the section on the three-dimensional composition of a building (illustration 9).

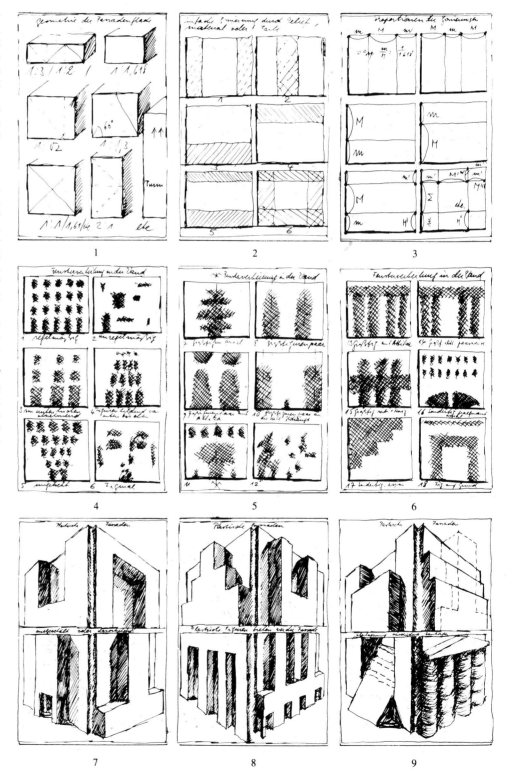

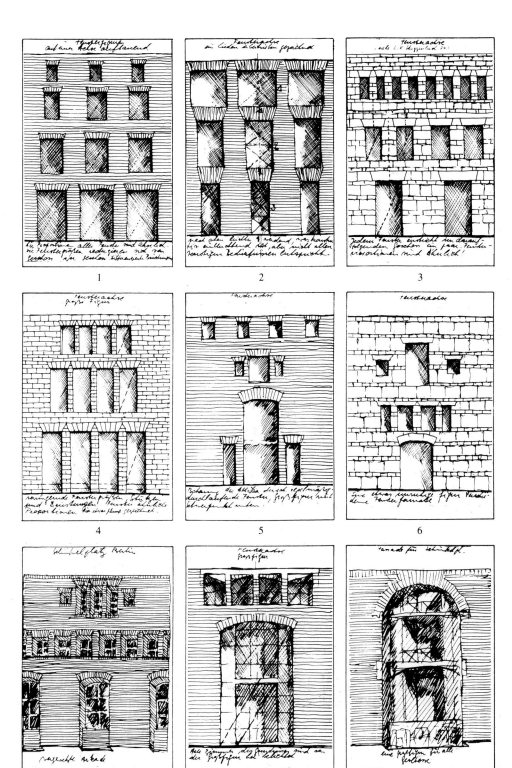

By means of the parts of elevations, shown here, the theme of facade figures running through vertically can be explained with examples.

Illustration 1: The distribution of windows is based on their axes. Similar window proportions are reduced in size storey. This motive underlines the perspective of the facade; it makes the building appear higher than it is in reality, and symbolises the need for more light penetration into the lower storeys of buildings in narrow streets.

Illustration 2: Here the windows increase in size which makes the facade appear lighter and symbolises its constructive logic.

Illustration 3: An almost 'mathematical' order is achieved by doubling the number of windows in each storey and by, at the same time, reducing their formats. Thus a very active facade provides nevertheless the same amount of opening space in each storey.

Illustration 4: Similar in appearance to the example shown in illustration 1, this figure, however, is not determined by the axes of the windows but by the grouping of windows together.

Illustration 5: A figure in an almost literal sense develops from this arrangement of windows, which is based on the coordination of different formats on one vertical axis. Here the emphasis lies on the entrance and the articulation of the attic by way of a regular series of equally sized windows.

Illustration 6: This somehow uneasy figure has a rather casual effect composed of different window formats. It is probably of importance at this point to again call one's attention to the spatial effects of interior rooms which can lead to such figuration on the facade.

Illustration 7: A projected base with regular openings (instead of pilasters), allows for the zone above to employ a new, independent, organisation of windows. This is a popular motive in 'big city' architecture, where the ground floor has a separate meaning. Adolf Loos applied this theme in his building at the Michaelerplatz in Vienna and the House of Tristan Tzara in Paris.

Illustration 8: One vertical element accumulates all necessary openings of the adjacent rooms. The two storey high glazing folds into the terraces, the middle section accommodating the sitting room and the sides of the bedrooms.

Illustration 9: The same figure as the only opening element in the facade; a gigantic figure wnich runs through all storeys. The scale of the building must be able to cope with such a monumental opening.

These examples no longer show only parts of the facade. Slender high buildings are demonstrated in their total composition and serve for each theme.

Illustration 1: A regular window composition based on axes. From bottom to top increasing sizes of windows culminate in a large-scale top floor.

Illustration 2: Clear separation into three zones: the ground floor with large-scale openings; a middle area with windows regularly distributed; and a light skeletal attic storey.

Illustration 3: Here the sizes of the windows are dimensioned in a way that the wall surfaces are largely reduced to 'piers' and 'beams'. However, because the window sizes vary in each storey, one cannot call this type a skeleton facade.

Illustration 4: The old theme of the 'piano nobile', the main floor of a house, is emphasised here by a closed attic zone.

Illustration 5: The exterior flights of stairs give the ground floor a public character. The large studio windows of the top floor indicate a clear difference in valuation compared with the small windows of the intermediate storey.

Illustration 6: A large-scale hall of columns, almost like a 'stoa', constitutes a powerful order which can also conceal the irregular and lively interior of the building.

Illustration 7: Elegant, slender window slits are bound together by a constructional arch, and form a figure with the circular windows of the attic storey. Thus a serial motive becomes an image.

Illustration 8: The zoning of this facade resembles the 'building block' principle, with its different surfaces and window partitions. It gives the impression of relatively independent storeys being piled up.

Illustration 9: Here we have an irregular facade structured according to the interior organisation of spaces. One should not underestimate the difficulty of distributing windows this freely, because it requires adherence to quite precise proportions relating the openings to one another. Excellent taste can lead to a harmonious yet free design, but a 'secret' principle of order is also the foundation of these kinds of composition.

1

2

3

4

5

6

Complete compositions are also shown in this plate. They cannot be applied arbitrarily, but can reinforce the whole 'tendency' of a building.

Illustration 1: The base is clearly distinguished from the rest of the building by having a different surface. Because of the terraces being cut out from the attic storey, the building has a battlement-like termination.

Illustration 2: This facade figure unfolds from the bottom to the top like a tree-top or a goblet. One may also find that the significance of the individual storeys diminishes towards the top.

Illustration 3: Here a plastic figure, a portico, projects from the building whereby the entrance is clearly emphasised.

Illustration 4: In contrast to illustration 2, the facade figure tapers off towards the top. Oddly enough, although the order is reversed, we do not perceive a change in meaning. Probably it is the hierarchical structure of the facade as such which suggests a hierarchy of significance.

Illustration 5: A projected arcade is sub-divided by a loggia on first floor level. A socially useful interspace is created, which almost gives the idea of theatrical staging.

Illustration 6: The gate motive in front of a largely glazed facade clearly demonstrates the problematic nature of the figure-ground relationship. The layering of the facade ranges from the opening of the gate, to the light background, until finally the surrounding frame of the building is reached.

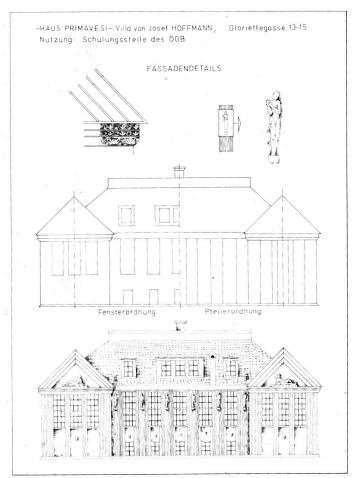

-HAUS PRIMAVESI- Villa von Josef HOFFMANN, Gloriettegasse 13-15
Nutzung: Schulungsstelle des ÖGB

FASSADENDETAILS

Fensterordnung          Pfeilerordnung

Manfred STÜRTZER
SCHÜTZENHAUS KAISERBAD

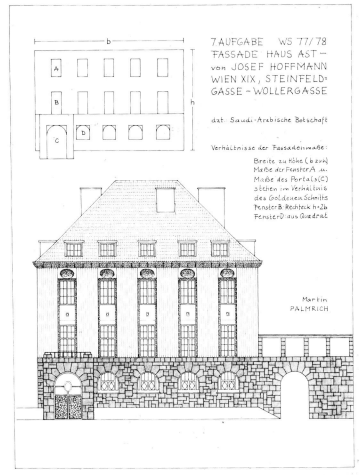

7.AUFGABE   WS 77/78
FASSADE HAUS AST—
von JOSEF HOFFMANN
WIEN XIX, STEINFELD=
GASSE – WOLLERGASSE

dzt. Saudi-Arabische Botschaft

Verhältnisse der Fassadenmaße:

Breite zu Höhe ( b zu h)
Maße der Fenster A u.
Maße des Portals(C)
stehen im Verhältnis
des Goldenen Schnitts
Fenster B: Rechteck h=2b
Fenster D: aus Quadrat

Martin
PALMRICH

Student works on the theme of Facades

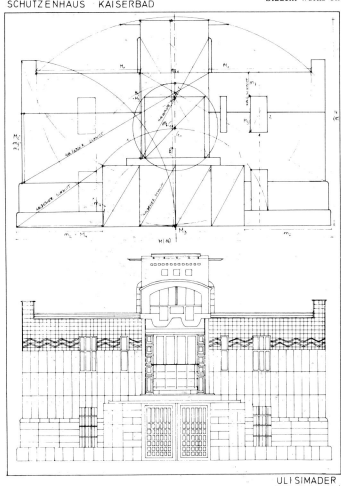

ULI SIMADER

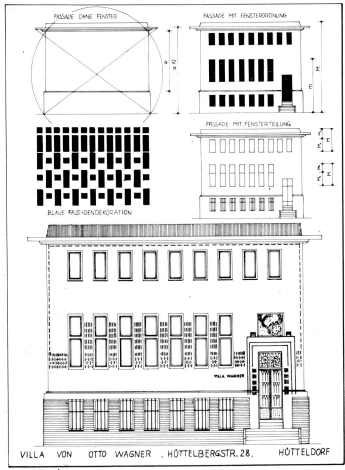

FASSADE OHNE FENSTER            FASSADE MIT FENSTERORDNUNG

BLAUE FASSADENDEKORATION        FASSADE MIT FENSTERTEILUNG

VILLA VON OTTO WAGNER , HÜTTELBERGSTR. 28,    HÜTTELDORF

WILHELM KÜHAS

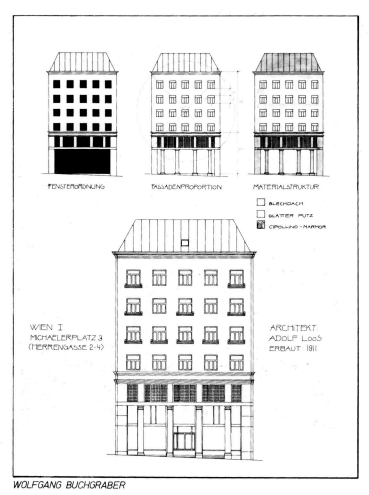

FENSTERORDNUNG     FASSADENPROPORTION     MATERIALSTRUKTUR

☐ BLECHDACH
☐ GLATTER PUTZ
▦ CIPOLLINO - MARMOR

WIEN I
MICHAELERPLATZ 3
(HERRENGASSE 2-4)

ARCHITEKT:
ADOLF LOOS
ERBAUT 1911

WOLFGANG BUCHGRABER

HAUS
SCHEU
WIEN XIII

M 1:200

FASSADE VERPUTZT
FENSTER VERGLAST
SPROSSEN WEISS LACKIERT

M 1:50

PROPORTION
GLIEDERUNG
FENSTERORDNUNG
FENSTERTEILUNG
MATERIAL

ARCH: ADOLF LOOS

WOLFGANG     SEDELMAIER

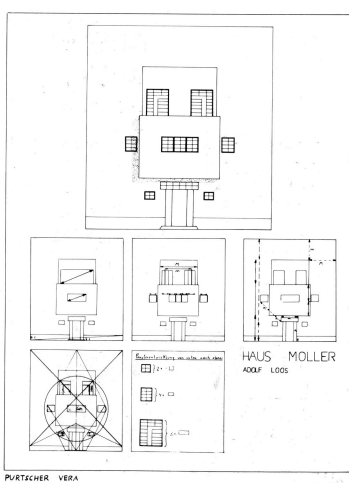

HAUS MOLLER
ADOLF LOOS

PURTSCHER VERA

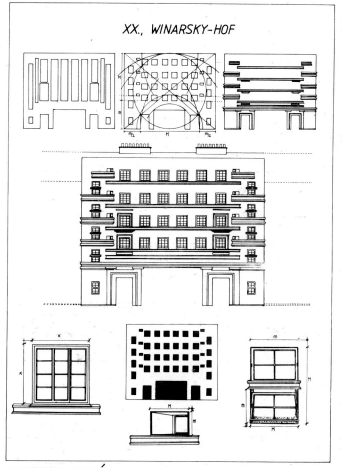

XX., WINARSKY-HOF

CHRISTIAN GAZSÓ

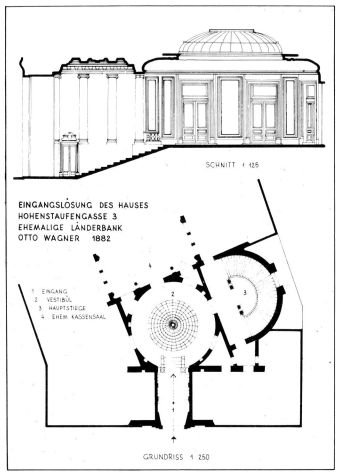

EINGANGSLÖSUNG DES HAUSES
HOHENSTAUFENGASSE 3
EHEMALIGE LÄNDERBANK
OTTO WAGNER   1882

1  EINGANG
2  VESTIBÜL
3  HAUPTSTIEGE
4  EHEM. KASSENSAAL

SCHNITT 1 125

GRUNDRISS 1 250

ERNST GFRERER

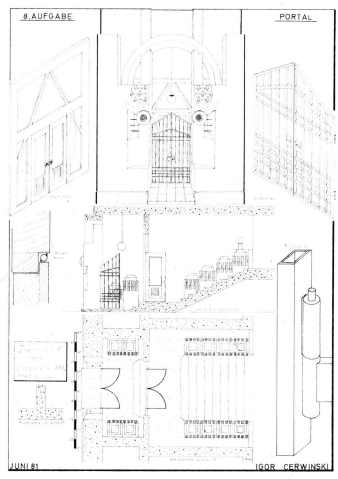

8. AUFGABE                    PORTAL

JUNI 81                       IGOR CERWINSKI

Student works on the theme of Entrances and Portals

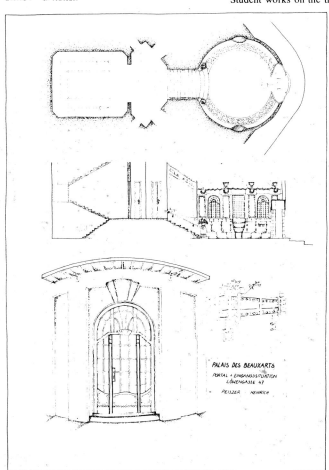

PALAIS DES BEAUXARTS
PORTAL + EINGANGSSITUATION
LÖWENGASSE 47

PELZER  HEINRICH

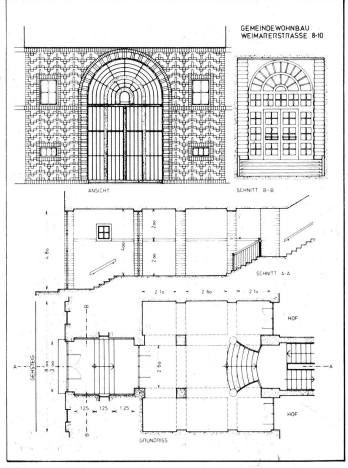

GEMEINDEWOHNBAU
WEIMARERSTRASSE 8-10

ANSICHT            SCHNITT B-B

SCHNITT A-A

GRUNDRISS

HÖRL  Christoph

# Entrances and Portals

On the way from the street into a building one passes through different graduations of what can be called 'the public'. Immediately, the position of the entrance and the architectonic significance it is given demonstrate the role and function of the building. Thus the main entrance of a large public building would not be a tiny hole located somewhere where nobody would find it. Equally it would be inappropriate for a modest house to be approached by a representational drive or large-scale flights of stairs.

The portal marks the transition from the public exterior to the private interior. It is an element of self-representation for the inhabitants. The route from the portal to the vertical means of access forms an individual space or series of spaces; this fact is much too seldom taken into account.

Portals and entrances have nowadays been mostly degraded to residual spaces. They merely suffice the requirements of building regulations. Uppermost in perversity is the combination of the entrance for vehicles—into a courtyard or underground car park—with the entrance into the building. For the pedestrian, only a narrow path along the wall is left. Thus, by passing the rubbish containers, one hurries to the safe apartment door, swearing at the dirty and devastated entrance; and what else can be expected from such a built reality?

Other bad examples are the so-called entrance halls of the modern centres of power; the office towers and insurance palaces. We find an open ground floor, flattened by the load of the ascending storeys, and awkwardly structured by wall partitions, greenery, mural pictures and orientation boards. Without all this crap, the entrance hall would be just an area without meaning. One should ask a visitor leaving one of these places whether or not he could remember the space. He would not even understand the question. For this reason the following examples have been chosen which clearly demonstrate the spatial qualities of entrance areas.

A notable example is the solution for the entrance to the former 'Länderbank' by Otto Wagner. The round vestibule, which is non-directional, acts as a distributor (illustration 1). Three different areas (banking hall, entrance and main staircase) are thus held together. A richly decorated art nouveau portal is pictured in illustration 2. As the actual door into the building is recessed, an ante-space is created which is made into a porch.

The next example (illustration 3) shows an interesting sequence of spaces. A round vestibule prepares the visitor for the following architectural event. A small flight of stairs narrows the space, which then opens into an irregular hexagon. After this landing, which is separated from the actual stairwell by wall projections, the route terminates in a staircase which ascends in three flights. There were times when even the entrance areas to blocks of council flats received the necessary design attention. This is clearly visible in the example of a Viennese 'Gemeindehaus' from the years between the wars (illustration 4). The portal is emphasised by a frame of bricks. A spacious porch opens into a proper vestibule with inviting bottom steps of a staircase and two doors; one giving access to the house, the other leading into the courtyard. Here a simple entrance has been turned into an enjoyable meeting place.

Veranda and staircase of a building in Resselgasse, Vienna, by J. Kornhäusel, early eighteenth century

Entrance hall of a bourgeois residential building, Vienna, c 1900

Vestibule of a building, Vienna, 1830

# Arcades

Who owns the arcades? Are they related to the street or the building? Or do they even belong to the pavement, creating its proper space? The arcade is determined by this ambivalence of application, but it is also an intermediate space which can be used and interpreted in many different ways. It can fulfill semi-public functions by being projected in front of a building whereby the user is neither outside nor inside the building. But the space of the arcade is also capable of assuming an independent public role. It can almost grow into the building behind, and thereby become an arcaded building. Finally there are examples where in the course of time, arcades have been filled in or walled up in order to gain additional space. (When old buildings are in the process of being restored, hidden arcades are often found behind plaster and brick walls.)

The arcade is a collective urban element. For its construction, it is necessary not only to gain the agreement of the neighbours in the particular street affected, but also to gain the permission, and even the instruction, of the building authorities. Once the arcade is built it becomes an individual urban element which is largely understood to be independent from the building behind. The reason why there are so few arcades built today is probably due to a lack of common sense when it comes to the determination of common urban elements. However, the usefulness and enrichment of the arcade for urban life has been proved for centuries.

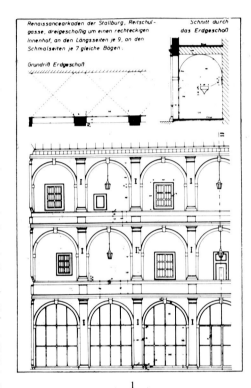

1

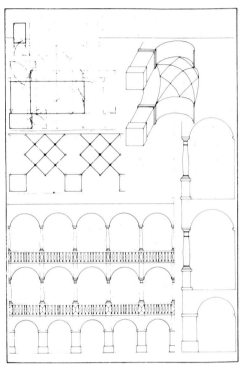

2

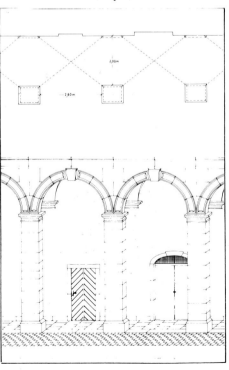

3

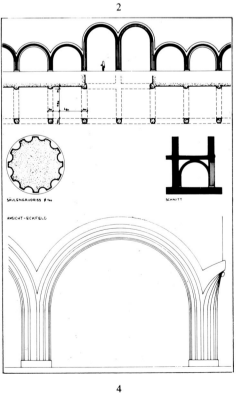

4

1

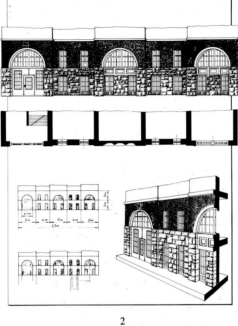

2

# Ground Floors

The base of a building, its ground floor zone, is without doubt the most important urban element of a facade. As it constitutes the transition to the ground, or the pavement, it is exposed to considerable strain, and therefore the material used for this zone is usually more durable than that used for the rest of the building.

The ground floor has a particular importance in urban life. Because this area is most directly perceived by people, it often serves for the accommodation of shops and other commerical enterprises. Given the nature of business, such a ground floor zone is also subjected to frequent change, especially in terms of its fittings. It is to be recommended therefore that the ground floor be given a robust, neutral structure which can cope with 'parasitical architecture' such as shop fittings. The examples here show different kinds of bases. They range from neutral backgrounds for large openings to buildings with a rejecting, even closed, character, whose ground floors do not, for some reason, have a public function.

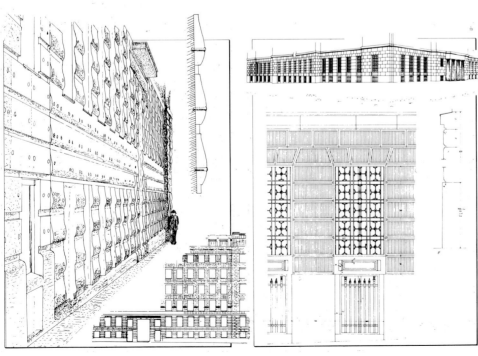

3                4

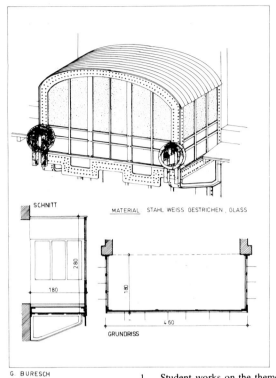

SCHNITT

MATERIAL STAHL WEISS GESTRICHEN, GLASS

280
180

180

GRUNDRISS

460

G. BURESCH

WOHNHAUS
WIEN 8, Lerchenfelderstraße 54
Verkleidung zwischen 2 & 3 St
aus Kupferblech
Säulen aus Marmor

SCHNITT

GRUNDRISS    II & III Stock

GERHARD RIEDLING

1    Student works on the theme of Bay-Windows, Balconies, Loggias    2

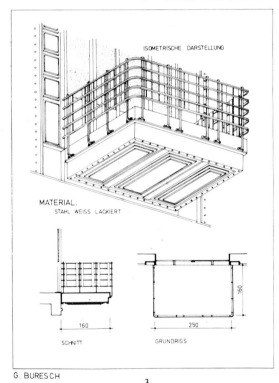

ISOMETRISCHE DARSTELLUNG

MATERIAL:
STAHL WEISS LACKIERT

160

160    250

SCHNITT    GRUNDRISS

G. BURESCH

3

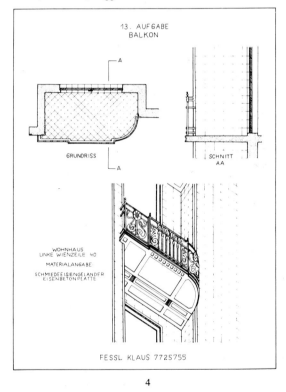

13. AUFGABE
BALKON

A

A

GRUNDRISS

SCHNITT
AA

WOHNHAUS
LINKE WIENZEILE 40

MATERIALANGABE

SCHMIEDEEISENGELANDER
EISENBETONPLATTE

FESSL KLAUS 7725755

4

# Bay-windows, Balconies and Loggias

Similar to arcades, bay-windows, balconies and loggias are to be seen as independent spatial units. They are in any case genuine enlargements of the apartment, providing a sense of stepping out of the building—out of the facade—although still being in the private realm. In addition to that, these elements allow for a better view of urban life; they open up 'new prospects' in the true sense of the word.

To a greater extent than the balcony, bay-windows and loggias also represent an enrichment of the interior space which lies behind, because they divide it into spaces of different value.

Another important argument in favour of bay-windows and loggias stresses their climatic function. They form a buffer zone to the exterior, which is of great advantage in terms of the energy consumption of the apartment. Experiments with winter gardens and projected conservatories have revealed interesting results which, although known long ago, were largely ignored in the recent period of energy wastage. After the last war, when only a few households were equipped with refrigerators, these parts of a building were often used for the storage of food during the winter. Even the intermediate space between double glazed windows also served for these purposes.

Two variants of bays are shown in illustrations 1 and 2. The bay-window in Otto Wagner's 'Schützenhaus' in Vienna (illustration 1) is conceived as a little building on its own; a pulpit above the river. Another building in Vienna reveals a bay element which vertically reaches over the entire facade creating the motive of a small building which is projectd from a large one (illustration 2). The two balconies shown in illustrations 3 and 4 are remarkable in terms of

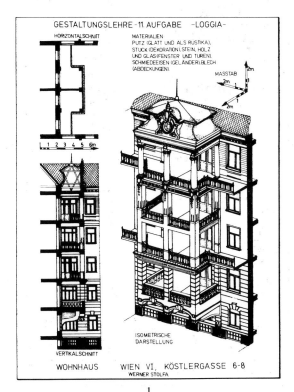

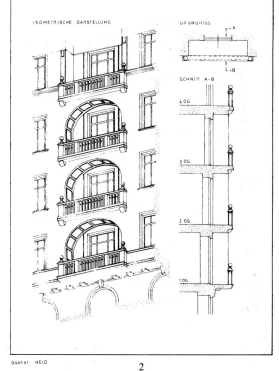

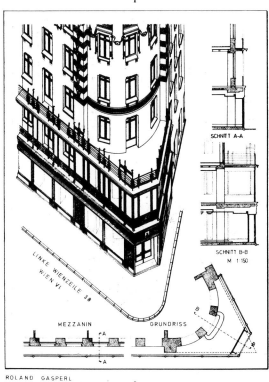

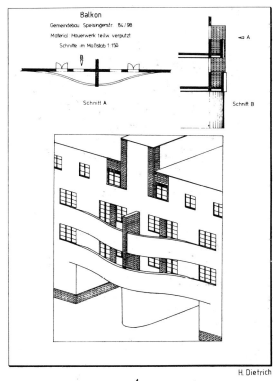

their painstaking, constructional treatment of the soffit.

Bay-windows, balconies and loggias are also very suitable for the functional structure of the facade. However, it goes without saying that these elements should not be distributed on the surface at random. I would recommend a concentration over several storeys, to allow for a further differentiation within these elements. This would also clearly increase the legibility of the different storeys.

The loggias shown in illustrations 1 and 2 are examples of representational building projections. The loggia in illustration 1 measures nearly three square metres and thereby almost resembles the size of a proper room. This clearly invites possible use as a room. In contrast to that, the arches dominating the loggias in illustration 2 constitute a representational frame, and more likely only invite the inhabitants to have a brief glance at the street. Probably here, the interior space is much more important, the loggia rather serving as an additional filter of the exterior. Especially at the times when the French windows are open would it suggest an optical enlargement of the room behind.

The degree to which these kinds of elements are also appropriate for the articulation of an impor-tant part of the building is shown in illustrations 3 and 4. The contour of a street corner is taken up again by the first two storeys of a corner building (illustration 3). But, as the angled rooms do not seem to be very suitable for apartments, the corner is interrupted by a cyclinder which provides space for a terrace and, in addition, monumentalises the corner of the building, especially when viewed from a distance. The big 'hole' in the facade of the 'Gemeindehaus' (illustration 4) achieves a positive meaning by way of curved balconies, which have the effect of the building mass being modulated.

# Roof and Attic Storey

Nowadays one apparently only comes across two types of roofs: the flat roof (the development and assessment of which does not need to be described here in detail), and the normal pitched roof, which by now has become wide-spread as the embodiment of the 'alpine style'. We should not engage ourselves in clichés, but rather look at the variety of possibilities and meanings that this important part of the building has, bearing in mind that it is a building's termination towards the sky. The meanings which language attaches to roofs are very instructive. For instance, if we reflect on the term 'roof landscape': it rises from the buildings like a skin and, overtopped by the higher silhouettes or public buildings, this artificial thing becomes a second plane between sky and earth. In general, the roof involves an ambiguous, undefined space which nowadays is mostly sacrificed to a radical exploitation of the building volume. But we should not completely forget this reservoir of secrets and memories. Here the objects of the past, the history of the inhabitants, and therefore that of the building itself are preserved.

For all this there is a simple explanation. The attic is a free place, a residual space, a store-room, a play area for children. It is often full of corners, mostly dark and dusty, the opposite of the exterior world. The roof is the crown of the building, the evidence of its meaning showing the pride and dignity of the building itself.

The crown is carried by the building body. Visually it is the termination of the facade, often with an attic storey inserted, by which device the roof is withdrawn from people's eyes. Therefore the top floor zone, the attic storey, is much more important for the design and composition of the facade than the actual roof.

The facade is protected from the weather by a cornice, or by any other projecting moulding. On top of these could be a small balustrade—as if there was a terrace behind—to hide the mysterious roof. At important points the attic storey is broken through by domes and towers which simply have the purpose of 'crowns'.

But let us return to the attic storey. The necessity of it being treated in a special way, in terms of form and function, results from the simple fact that a building has a top and a bottom. The bottom is the base which has to communicate its particular relationship with the earth. At the top everybody should know that the building ends there.

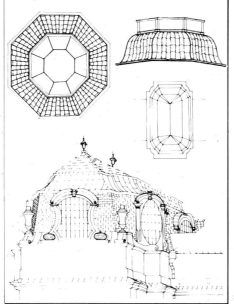

Student works on the theme of Roofs and Attics

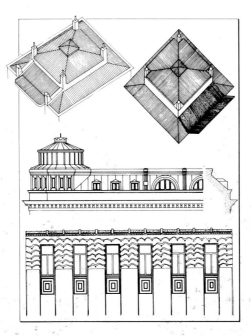
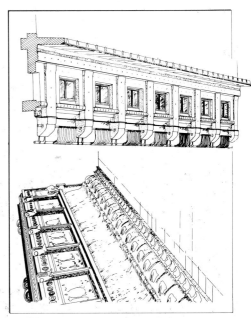

Basilica in Vicenza, by A. Palladio, 1546—49

Cathedral in Ferrara, after 1135

Bourgeois residential building at Dannebergplatz, Vienna

Castello Sforzesco in Milan

'Ankerhaus' in Graben, Vienna, by O' Wagner, 1895

Palm House in the 'Burggarten', Vienna, F. Ohmann, c 1900

# Ground-Plan and Building Form

A long-standing error in contemporary architecture is the belief that there is a logical connection between the function and the form of a building; or even that the latter is a result of the former. But as this irrevocable equation of a direct analogy of function and space, or form, is non-existent, an attempt was made to create an auxiliary theory which ended in a diffused, vague definition and vindication of architecture. Seemingly the infinite possibilities which lie in the relationship of function and form were not understood in a positive way. No ground-plan or building can be traced back directly to a function. Always in architecture, certain 'types of spaces' will be applied. They are ultimately relatively independent from the initially required function which existed at the beginning of the planning process.

Therefore let us assume that the design of a building develops from the interdependence of the requirements of the users—the functions—and the types of spaces which are provided by architecture. Requirements alone do not make a building. If so, all doors would be opened to 'hypertrophic ferocity' and the disruption of buildings.

The majority of functions and ground-plans are easily capable of being related to simple types if the rules and procedures of function are understood. Within itself, every type provides enough freedom of design. Experience shows that with the clarity and simplicity of the ground-plan, and the form of a building, the possibilities of different uses increase.

Quite frequently, the argument is put forward that confinement to precise building types would restrict the individuality of architectural design. But it is exactly this excessive individuality which leads to the nowadays much lamented wildness in architecture and its lack of conception.

In contrast, the examples which follow show the possibilities of individual differentiation of buildings with similar ground-plans. An additional aid in the design of a building is the analysis of the topographical and typological situation of the surroundings, and the tradition of the respective area. In principle, one should always presume that every site has its own social and historical meaning. To discover, and to investigate, its implications is a pre-condition for the cultural understanding of an architectural design. Every place has its specific conditions and its history. People have given meaning to even the most desolate prairie, the seemingly untouched desert, and the most inaccessible mountain areas. Legends and myths do exist, and

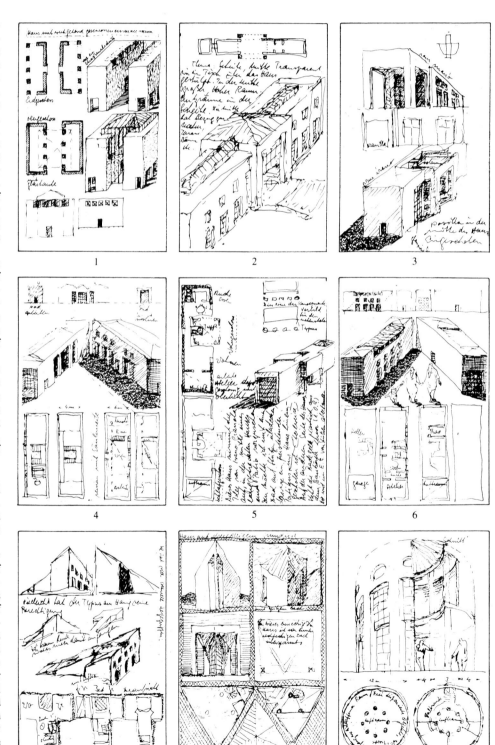

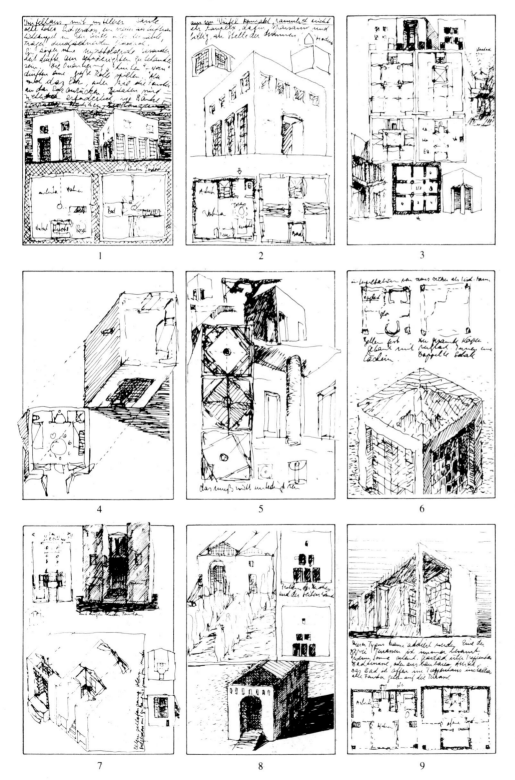

1          2          3

4          5          6

7          8          9

certain places evoke associations for many people. No place is a virgin piece of land.

The choice of the building type and the building form is dependent on these general specific conditions, which mean more than mastering the requirements of a building's future inhabitants and its architectural possibilities. Without taking into account the complex situation of a particular site, a building is merely a trivial throw-away product; and without the involvement of the cultural heritage, every solution remains individualistic and idle arbitrariness.

The art of architecture, the decision on the building type and the design of the building itself, begin with the deliberate superimposition of the conditions of the place with the requirements of the inhabitants. If he takes these pre-conditions seriously, every honest architect will therefore quickly consider a simple, understandable and appropriate building type.

## Development and Composition

Every ground-plan should be conceived and developed in relation to space. Here, very often from the client's side, the first obstacles to understanding occur, because he is normally not experienced in spatial imagination. But there is a useful rule of thumb which might help in this situation: at the beginning of a building process, the architect should never confuse or overwhelm the client. Simple geometrical basic forms also provide sufficient possibilities for spatial surprise. This kind of discipline excludes much unnecessary estrangement, because it involves concrete experience and understanding.

Then the work on the form of the building can be started. Once its rough contours are visible, the requirements of refining become the next step. Openings are brought into a rhythm, and are combined to form a motive; exterior spaces, such as terraces, balconies or loggias are added, not as missing pieces, but as a kind of second layer to the building.

The most important problem when designing a building is probably the determination of the line which has to be drawn between interior and exterior space. At this point, the whole range of possibilities of how to create an appropriate transition from the private sphere to the public realm comes into question. A change in conception occurs whereby these two different spaces have to be taken into consideration. In contrast to a much cherished ideology of architects advocating the unlimited transition of interior and exterior, the user in general knows very well where to draw the line between these spaces.

# Square Buildings

For the study of simple geometrics related to the conception of residential buildings, I would like first of all to talk about the square. The following three plates will deal with this basic form and will show how it allows for the manipulation of the space within. The most decisive question which arises when designing square rooms is probably what to do with the centre; whether to fill it in or to keep it void. The square Roman house has its fireplace exactly in the centre, whereas the entrance was of minor importance, and therefore situated in a corner of the building.

As a geometrical object, the cube most clearly communicates the notion of enclosure and also the symbol of stability. The cube therefore, among the Platonic solids, symbolizes the earth.

The sub-divisions and fragmentations shown in the following plates should first of all be understood independently of function and use. They simply state principal formal possibilities which give rise to definable rules of how to solve the conflict of enclosure and division, and, by way of interior structure, how spatial effects are changed.

To commence the sequence we can consider the all-round enclosure, which is orientated towards the centre, where the similarity of division is emphasised by a pier (illustrations 1 and 2). Spatial focus is mainly determined by the position of the staircase. This is the case in the building shown in illustration 3 despite the living areas running through. Illustration 4 demonstrates the superimposition of a circulation axis with a central staircase, by which device the centre of the building is clearly determined. Illustration 5 concerns a directional division, by which the building is subdivided into two, or several, zones representing different spatial valuations. A common practice is to sub-divide the building into a main zone and two subsidiary zones (illustration 6), whereby the main space can have its own geometry to emphasise its particular position. The interior fragmentation of a solid appears in illustration 7. The square remains by way of its bordering lines, but in terms of its interior, it allows for complete freedom of spatial arrangement. Thus the square is left recognisable only when viewed from the outside.

Illustrations 8 and 9 show examples of one-directional space. One side of the square is accentuated by a large opening and thus constitutes the main side, the facade, of the building.

The centralized vertical arrangement within a cube is divided into quarter segments, each of which starts at a different height (illustration 1). The shape of the square is repeated in the gap between the stairs in the central well. This method is also applied in principle in the next example (illustration 2), where the centre is constituted by an atrium.

As with all other simple geometrical forms, the square can also be superimposed on other forms. Illustration 3 shows a cube being cut through yet having a central hall. The contrast between solid and amorphous basic forms, that is between hard and soft, results in exciting spaces (illustration 4).

Different forms within a composition appear to be punched out (illustration 5), whereby the residual spaces—with walls of different thickness—disregard the overall shape of the enclosure.

The disintegration of the square, taking place step by step, is shown in illustrations 6 and 9. Only piers remain of the basic geometrical form. Thus a second spatial layer develops, which is useful for the mediation of interior and exterior.

The square in general, being a neutral and non-directional basic form, asks for dialectical contrasts, like a frame which surrounds changing images. So the inner spaces themselves can be created as geometrical forms, or they can follow the lines of movement within a building.

A special form of the square is constituted by the loosening of its sides and by the accentuation of its four corners. Massive corner towers define a transparent interior space (illustration 1), or are reduced to bay-like projections from a solid core (illustration 2). The co-existence of two different building forms is achieved by the surrounding cube being fragmented, whereby the solid form lying behind becomes visible (illustrations 3 and 4). A variation of this type is shown in illustration 5. A central cylinder serves as the main space and at the same time as a distributor, giving access to the corner towers each of which have different spatial geometries.

Le Corbusier also concerned himself with the square. Illustration 6 shows a studio building which reveals a poetic structure. The next example (illustration 7) suggests a central core from which very different spatial divisions are possible without destroying the overall form of the building.

The sketches in illustrations 8 and 9 are attempts at structuring a square facade. As already mentioned in the section on facades, the geometrical reality of a facade can, by way of visual manipulations, develop into one with a different effect.

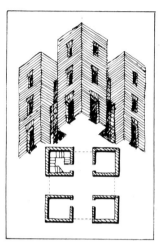

1

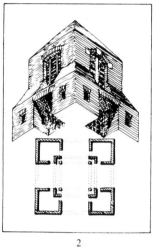

2

3

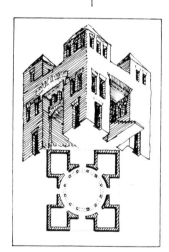

4

5

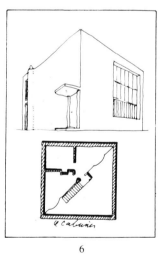

6

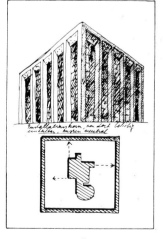

7

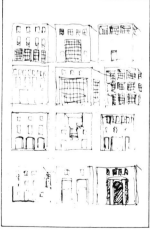

8

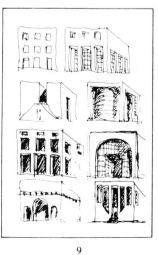

9

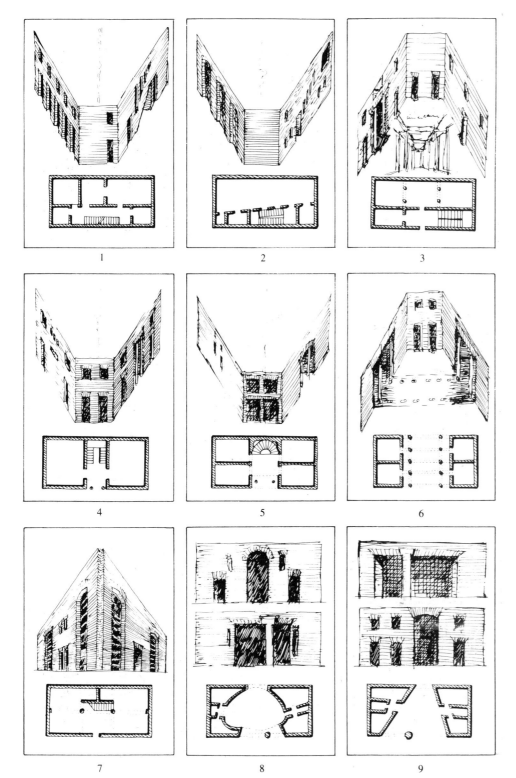

1     2     3

4     5     6

7     8     9

# Rectangular Buildings

Rectangular ground-plans are clearly directional; the extension of the rectangle therefore has certain effects on the division of the ground-plan. Also, the building has a clear direction of movement which influences the way it is used, unless this direction of movement is terminated by sub-divisions and—above all—by the position of the staircase.

Another aspect of rectangular ground-plans affects the design of the building itself. The different valuation given to the facades on the long and the short sides can hardly be changed by means of composition. That means that here the possibilities of design are limited.

One possibility of the typological structuring of a rectangular building is to situate the staircase in parallel with a long side (illustrations 1 to 3). By so doing, a longitudinal zone is created which separates main and subsidiary spaces from each other.

If the long sides have a centre, the building is automatically divided into two halves (illustrations 4 to 6). Thus a staircase in the centre makes possible the division of the whole into two spaces of equal value (illustration 4). These can be further sub-divided (illustration 5). With a central hall running through vertically (illustration 6), this kind of division is even more distinct.

The examples of this plate show superimpositions of solid and skeletal building parts. Columns are never only constructional elements, as they always create an independent spatial layer or an additional ordering factor to the structure of a space. Therefore the rhythm of piers has to be well-considered.

In illustration 1 we have an interior structure which is constituted by piers and pilasters. This sub-division almost directly provokes a certain valuation and use of the spaces created; main and subsidiary spaces become obvious.

The examples in illustrations 2 and 4 show the fragmentation of rectangular solids by way of projected loggias. In illustration 5 the middle part of a building is loosened to become a central hall, the two remaining corner towers forming prominent terminations to the building.

A lively combination of solid and skeleton building parts ensues if they are superimposed (illustration 6). The result of this method is that two different rectangular structures seem to be integrated with one another.

In illustrations 7 and 8 these two principles of defining a space simply co-exist. The first example (illustration 7) shows a solid part juxtaposed with a hall of piers, whereas in the second example (illustration 8) the constructional possibilities of solid and skeleton are deliberately opposed.

Finally, the rectangular solid can also be understood as a container which accommodates a free form (illustration 9).

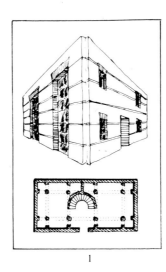

1

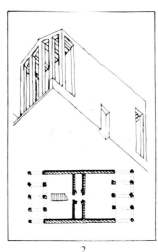

2

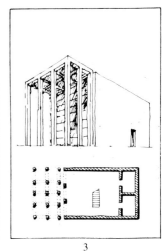

3

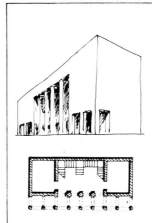

4

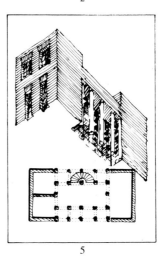

5

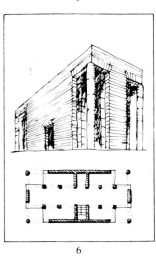

6

# T-shaped Ground-Plans

This type offers manifold possibilities of interpretation. It can be a centralised building with three extensions, a longitudinal building with an accentuated centre, or even the combination of four centralised buildings forming a T-shape.

One realises that it is the projecting part of the building which constitutes the real challenge for the design of this building type: is it a triumphant portico projecting from the facade; is it simply an extension on the back; or are the two side wings merely extensions of a centralised building? It is clear that the particular building parts have to be treated very carefully according to their valuation. Otherwise the intended meaning can easily turn into its opposite.

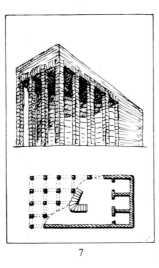

7

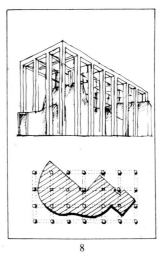

8

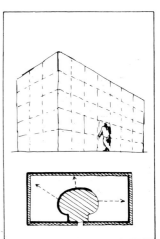

9

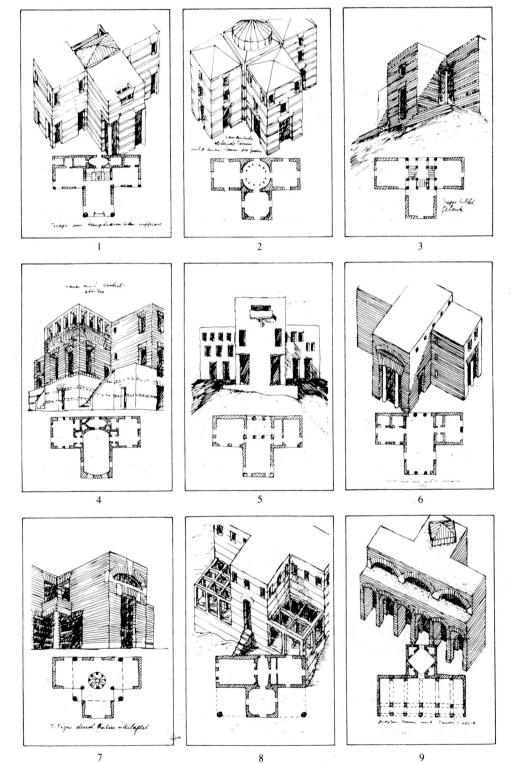

1

2

3

4

5

6

7

8

9

The projecting part of the building in illustration 1 seems to result from a need for additional space. The long side accommodates all subsidiary rooms and the entrance; and the staircase pushes the 'middle' part out towards the front. The next example (illustration 2) consists of four individual solids, whereby the central dark one functions as the element of access to the building. It is also the central part in illustration 3 which gives access to the building. The side wings are distinguished from it by way of transparent joints.

The building in illustration 4 is divided in transverse direction due to the arrangement of the subsidiary rooms. The central part is clearly the main space. This kind of division is also applied in the following examples (illustrations 5 and 6). However, the main space here is even more articulate.

The simple method of superimposing the T-shape with a square potentially allows one to get rid of the dark zones constituted by the inner corners (illustration 7). The exterior piers of the loggias determine the form of the square; the walls the T-shape. If the exterior space is filled with pergolas (illustration 8), the whole complex is supplemented to become a rectangle on plan. This shows that through architectural treatment of residual spaces it is possible to gain complete building forms. In contrast to that, we see in illustration 9 one building part being almost separated, as the longitudinal principal part is especially emphasised. Because of the entrance by way of the tower-like building part, it receives a centre.

# T-shaped Ground-Plans

Within the main space, a row of piers creates a filter in front of a tower which is a kind of annexe (illustration 1). A transverse main space is emphasised by the dissolution of the side wings (illustration 2). The massive corners of the longitudinal parts of a building (illustration 3), give the space in the middle its direction. This is broken by a light loggia projecting from the building. This type has been built as a four room maisonette apartment in my project for Ritterstrasse in Berlin. The direction of the main space of the building shown in illustration 4 is clearly visible.

The enclosed rectangle can have a projected pergola. In illustrations 5 and 6 we see the solid parts of two buildings being shrunk into a core. In both examples the T-shape is only constituted by piers.

A building with an opposite development is shown in illustration 7. The core is entirely dissolved by a transparent staircase tower, and by isolation from the other three towers.

If the T-shape is superimposed with a circular or semi-circular cylinder (illustrations 8 and 9), which can also be designed as monumental main spaces, the projections recede to become merely emphasised entrances.

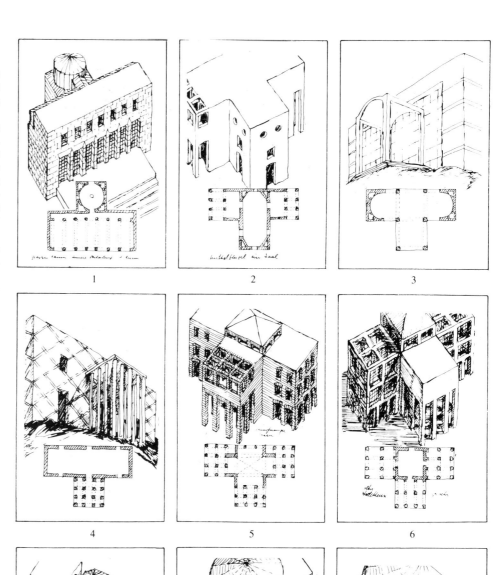

1  2  3

4  5  6

7  8  9

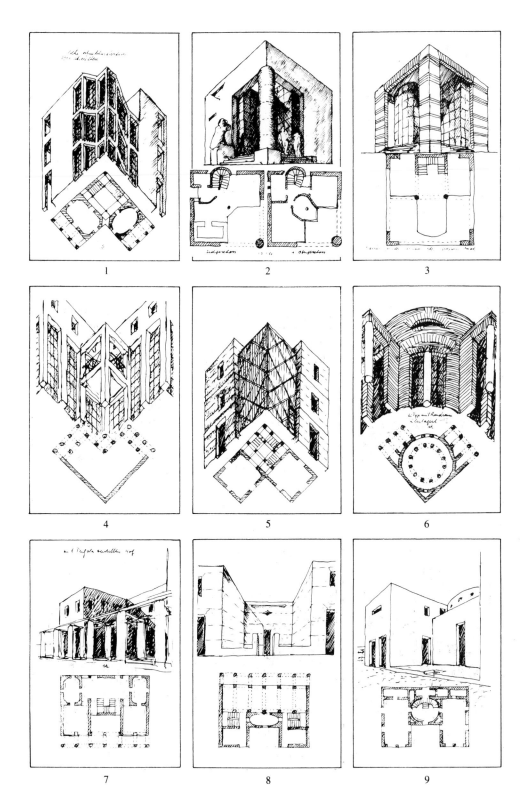

1

2

3

4

5

6

7

8

9

## L-Types

L-shaped ground-plans are especially suitable for arrangements of buildings because of the protected free space which is created between them. The examples shown here are geometrical types developed from a square, a quarter of which has been left void. They differ from the functionalist L-type, where the living area is situated in the shorter wing and the bedrooms are joined together in the longer one. The disadvantage of L-shaped building types lies in the possibility of dark corners at the junction. It is advisable to use this space for subsidiary rooms or staircases.

Illustration 1 shows an example where the staircase is located in the joint, the space in the wings having loggias in front. The superimposition of L-form and the square gives rise to the exterior space being fixed (illustrations 2 and 3). In the next example the edge consists of massive walls (illustration 4), whereas the open sides are relieved by piers. Illustration 5 represents an assemblage of independent building elements. A transparent tower accommodating the staircase is flanked by two solid towers. The next example shows an L-form being superimposed with a cylinder, which becomes the dominating figure of the building. The two wings are built as verandas.

## U-Types

These building forms still inevitably have a masterly character. The distinct symmetry with its defined centre is so dominant that a mitigation by way of fragmentation or similar techniques is difficult to achieve. Illustration 7 shows this classic type.

Its retracted courtyard is closed by a pergola. The opposite effect is gained if a pergola constitutes the long side of a building (illustration 8). By this, the transverse main space is clearly defined, the two wings being left to accommodate the subsidiary rooms. In illustration 9 the long side of the building is terminated by a buffer zone with subsidiary spaces. The centre is dominated by a staircase, and the side wings accommodate two main spaces.

# Building Corners

The corner of a building is one of the most important zones and is mainly concerned with the mediation of two facades. During the past decades this subject in architecture has been largely neglected. Nowadays, as a result of simply lining up buildings, the corner as a particular part of the building has not received the necessary acknowledgement and treatment.

In contrast to this, the following sketches should demonstrate some possibilities for special corner treatment. The first example shows (illustration 1) that the corner has also been dealt with in modern architecture. Guiseppe Terragni and the Russian constructivist Golosov achieved similar results by emphasising the corner of a building by way of a glass cylinder. This solid carries the architrave of the top storey like a huge, dematerialised round column. The turning of the corner is especially emphasised by a projecting frame which marks the actual termination of the building (illustration 2). In illustration 3 the psychological shearing off the corner is counteracted by way of an inserted pyramid, a sensitive but perhaps too powerful a protection of the corner. The rounded, retracted corner

1

2

3

4

5

6

7

8

9

shown in illustration 4 is emphasised by a similarly shaped row of columns creating a filter and reducing the dark zone often associated with a deep corner. In illustration 5 the corner is formed as a building in its own right—a tower. The problem of connecting the tower with the street facades is solved by the employment of loggias. Illustrations 6 and 7 also present corner towers which in terms of their proportions are to be regarded as classical solutions.

The curve, the circle and the turning of a corner are, in formal terms, logical means of protecting a corner. Parts and elements of the facade, without being broken, can thereby be 'wound round' from one facade to the next. The tower allows for a proper termination of the side facades and creates an additional accentuation.

The emptying of a corner or, in other words, a corner being opened up is shown in illustration 8. The small monument with its outward edges takes up the alignment of the two adjacent facades. The example presented in illustration 9 is a useful solution both in constructional and functional terms: the stepped form and the dissolution into pergolas allow for a positive response to the otherwise large dark zone of a corner. By opening the corner towards the top such problems are removed.

1

2

3

4

5

6

7

8

9

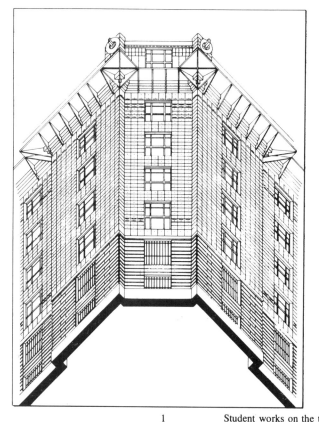

1

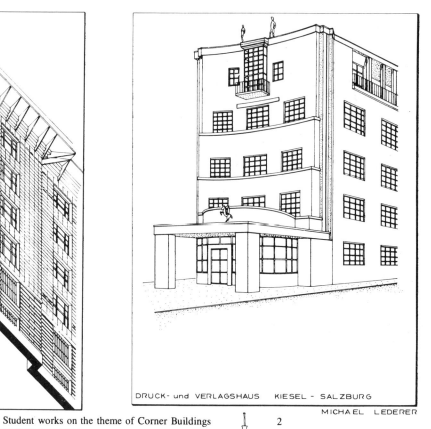

DRUCK- und VERLAGSHAUS    KIESEL - SALZBURG

MICHAEL LEDERER

2

Student works on the theme of Corner Buildings

Matthias MULITZER

3                                                                                                4

Illustration 1: A masterly achievement in terms of the most subtle and yet accentuated development of a corner is realised in Otto Wagner's Post Office Savings Bank in Vienna. The surfaces of the last vertical window axis of the side facades are drawn forward and stand out almost like a frame, terminated by the bevelled corners above. The setback also accommodates a vertical window axis and signals the development of a diagonal prospect from the building. Three elements, the two vertical parts of the 'frame' and the corner itself are held together by a projecting cornice, the consoles of which constitute the point of transition of the different parts. All this prepares finally for the corner to be crowned by a tower.

Illustration 2: A ground-plan level pavilion in front of a building corner completes the alignment of the two facades which approach each other at an acute angle. The actual corner facade, which is slightly concave and terraced towards the top, recedes. The setbacks of the storeys end at top floor level which is emphasised by a window situated in the vertical axis, and is crown-

Zentralsparkasse und Kommerzbank Stephansplatz

ERWIN HANDLER

1

WOLFGANG BUCHGRABER

2

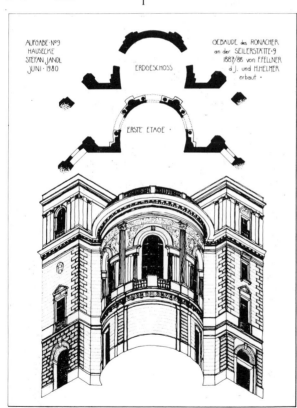

AUFGABE·Nº9 HAUSECKE STEFAN JANDL JUNI·1980

ERDGESCHOSS

ERSTE ETAGE·

GEBAUDE des RONACHER an der SEILERSTATTE·9 1887/88 von F.FELLNER d.J. und H.HELMER erbaut·

3

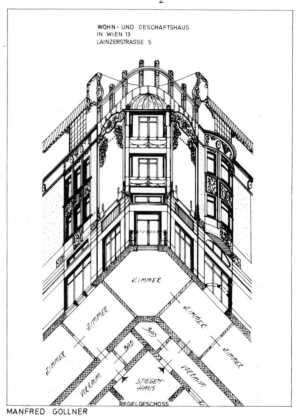

WOHN- UND GESCHÄFTSHAUS IN WIEN 13 LAINZERSTRASSE 5

MANFRED GOLLNER

4

ed by two statues. In addition, this corner is separated from the side facades by way of recessed corners.

Illustration 3: This building shows the transparency of mediation of different building levels. The entrance area reaches symmetrically right round the corner and, by way of a wall band above, is connected with the side facades. The plaster joints at the end of the side facades mark their termination. The loggias finally allow the bevelled corner to widen towards the top whereby a plane is created. This is flanked by two flag-staffs, which help evince the corner as being a complete form.

Illustration 4: This example shows the penetration of a corner. One side penetrates the other and develops into an expressive gateway structure. The small balconies at the corner do not represent the prolongation of the facade, but the penetration of the corner.

WALTER LEXMÜLLER     1     Student works on the theme of Interior Courtyards     2     JOHANNES ZIESER

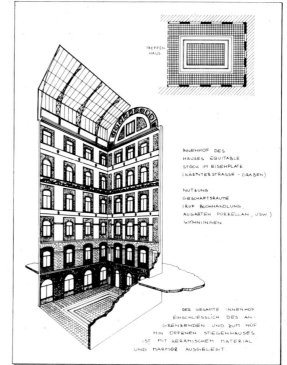

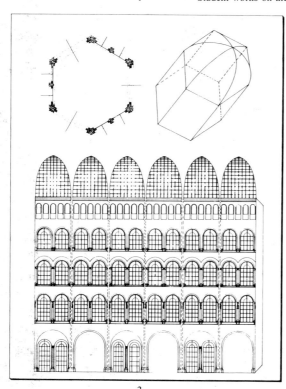

3                     4

# Interior Courtyards

Interior courtyards are not independent elements, but the outcome of a certain kind of building. We should not concern ourselves here with original historical and rural forms of this type, so the 'atrium' and other similar types of courtyard buildings will not be at issue. What will be dealt with in this context are examples of courtyards as they are found in cities. Courtyards are semi-public spaces which are for the use of the community concerned. They can also be part of an informal route network of passages and thoroughfares which give access to various parts of the city (illustrations 1 and 3). A large roofed courtyard, a hall so to speak, is especially useful in public buildings as a device of orientation. It also removes the tightness of an office complex and allows for additional ventilation and illumination (illustration 2). As a residential courtyard within an urban development (illustration 4), the courtyard is a common space used by the inhabitants of the adjacent buildings. Especially because of excessive traffic, the streets and therefore public life are often restricted in cities; the courtyard has thus gained a new significance. Today one should strive to locate apartments orientated towards a quiet courtyard rather than towards the street. This is a development which is only beginning but which will result in greater support for, and consideration of, existing and new interior courtyards. The required changes to traditional building types must, however, be made sense of.

Interior courtyard between Wollzeile and Bäckerstrasse, Vienna

Vista between Lerchenfelderstrasse and Neubaugasse in Vienna, nineteenth century

Palais Epstein in Vienna by Th. von Hansen, 1870—75

Courtyard in the Justizpalast in Vienna, by A. Wielemanns, 1875—81

# Outside Staircases

As the term already explains, outside staircases form part of the exterior space. They are human structures of landscape. They also act as markers in natural and urban environments, and communicate their public use. We can think for example of a large Baroque outside stair which, although related to an axis, also leads away from it and therefore engenders moments of contemplation. Another example is a footpath in the countryside. If simply made steps emerge in hilly terrain then we know that this path is often used by people, and that it facilitates walking.

Beyond this, outside staircases also create their own space, become points of encounter, meeting places, or simply points from which beautiful views can be enjoyed. I think it is not necessary to enlarge upon the fact that these characteristics have largely been lost, and have been substituted by the simplistic idea of the 'shortest connection between two points'.

Illustration 1 shows a simple straight staircase cut into the upper level of a building. Already at the bottom level, one comes under the influence of the upper level because of the stair. One can then slowly ascend it. However, the degree to which a staircase is projected from its upward termination (illustrations 2 and 3) determines the different possible relationships between the two levels. If our sense of spatiality was still intact, we would realise the difference.

What we nowadays experience instead is somebody rushing up the stairs and getting confused because, as is shown in illustration 4, one staircase often turns at right angles into two.

Staircases which run parallel to one another (illustration 5) give every level an independent, yet equal significance. This arrangement resembles terraces. Illustration 6 shows an almost semi-circular staircase running up in three flights suggesting a slope. Stairs which separate and come together again have a special character because of the way they are used by the public (illustration 7). People meet and separate again; they can time their walking speed either to encounter others or to avoid them. One could almost call this an example of 'freedom of use'. Illustration 8 shows an interesting though special form. A stair rises like a spiral and at the same time it narrows. From the beginning, the user becomes aware that the stair is going to end at a certain point. The example presented in illustration 9 again shows a cut-in staircase which is now curved and runs parallel to the upper level.

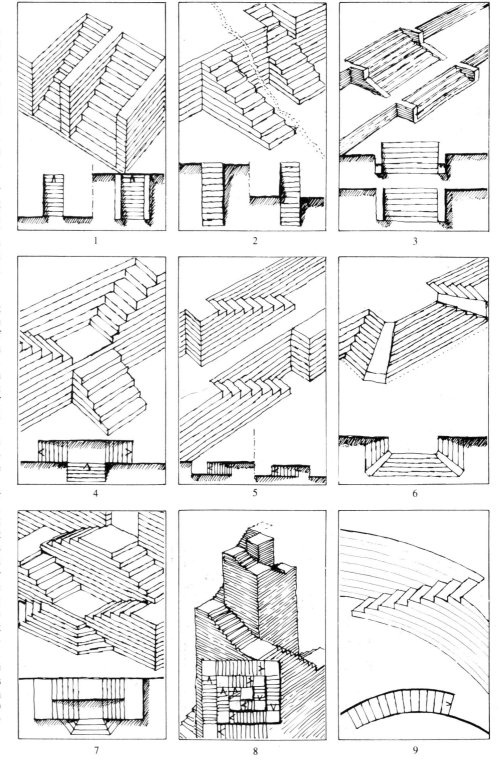

1

2

3

4

5

6

7

8

9

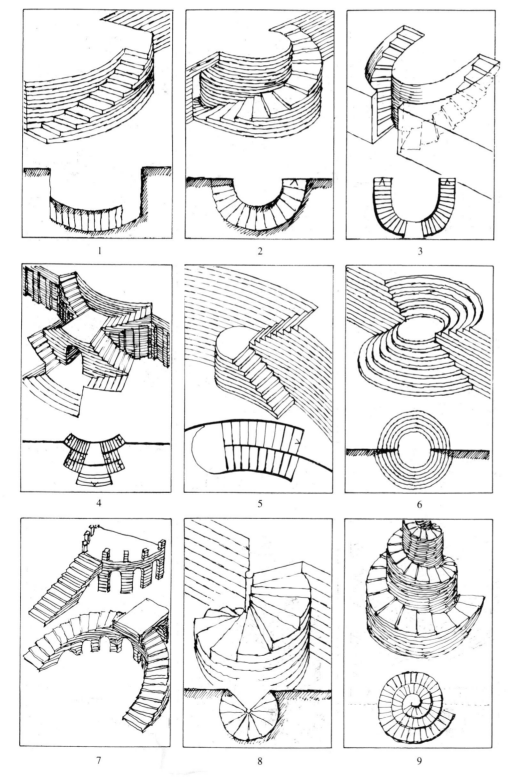

1

2

3

4

5

6

7

8

9

Illustration 1 represents the opposite effect of that gained in illustration 9 on the former plate. Here the curved form of the stair gives the impression that the upper level has a greater significance than in the example before.

The semi-circular staircase shown in illustration 2 emerges from a particular level to lead up to the next one. Initially one moves away from it to come back to it again on another level. The next example considers a staircase which is again cut into the ground (illustration 3). Only after having moved on to the bottom step has one really left the area concerned. A bold variation of opposite staircases is shown in illustration 4. The division into main levels and intermediate landings is striking. The following staircase (illustration 5) also possesses an intermediate landing. From half way up one has already entered the sphere of the upper level. This effect of an 'exterior' and 'interior' to a staircase is even more explicit in the simple, yet in another way sophisticated, arrangement shown in illustration 6. One half of the stair is 'heaped up', the other half 'cut in'. Apart from the variety of possible lines of movement and connection, the circular intermediate landing clearly manifests a meaningful centre. Examples of representational front staircases are presented in illustration 7. Here the upper level clearly has the prominent meaning. A rare example for an exterior stair is a spiral staircase (illustration 8). As a 'functional winding' it is a pre-runner—or maybe a result—of the Tower of Babel, even more reminiscent in the last example (illustration 9).

# Prospect

With the issue of the prospect, although it is closely related to architecture, we leave the subject 'building' as an independent subject of design and set out to think about public space. It has already been hinted at that the obligation of every building is to be integrated into its specific urban tissue. A special problem in this context is presented by the 'prospect'.

Let us take the common case that a street or a square is to be terminated by a building—our building. This termination is not to be treated as an accident; the facade of the building concerned has to react to this specific situation. While the street as such is a symbol of infinity, its termination communicates the fact that a destination has been reached. This destination, the facade of our building, must respond to this event, must catch the eye; only then will the building make sense and be integrated into the urban context. If we are committed to our responsibility for urban space, we have to respect its laws. That we have regard to the effect of prospects has nothing to do with a deliberate monumentalization of buildings, but with rendering respect to the urban texture. A prospect at the end of a street makes the eye rest, gives it a target, and thereby symbolically shortens the way to the destination.

By taking into consideration the effect our facade has on adjacent street alignments, we communicate our concern for the rules of the place where we build. We should not make people think about our building in the sense that a space ship has landed in their town by accident. What we should care about is giving evidence that we are going to continue to build more for this specific, for our, place.

# Towers and Monuments

Building is always about the occupation of a place. Architecture is about setting marks. In the free countryside we come across a tower. It directs our way. Lighthouses, chimneys, steeples, city gates, defence towers etc. belong to the archetypal symbols of uprightness. Towers symbolize the existence of human achievement, the triumph over earthly matters. Without doubt every tower has a monumental character as it rises above the environment. Having said that I can see before

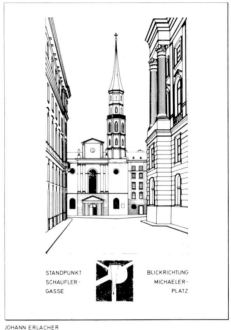

JOHANN ERLACHER

Manfred STURTZER

1    Student works on the theme of Prospect    2

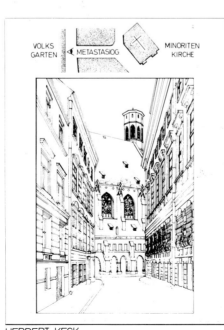

HERBERT KECK    3

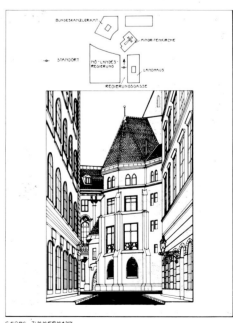

GEORG ZIMMERMANN    4

1

2

3

4

5

6

7

8

9

my inner eye certain modern architects shaking a warning finger at me. Monumentality? If one dares to talk about this last taboo of the Moderne, one is too easily accused of having a longing for a totalitarian state of affairs. What a stupid and short-sighted fallacy! A monument is of course first and foremost a sign of power. Only the mighty potentate could afford to rise above his subjects by way of architectural manifestations. But he is mortal, whereas his monument will outlast him and will be celebrated by future generations as a cultural testimony. Without these 'signs of power' there would be no such thing as architecture; we would dwell in a desolate steppe.

Monuments always were, and still are, cult objects which have meaning and value for a community. Because of their symbolism, they express a common will or confession. Monuments do not need to be towers or high-rise buildings. A small wayside shrine at the forking of a route suffices as a sign of human existence. But let us try again and find out what the term 'monumentality' really means. It certainly implies a lasting piece of architecture; it also conveys the beauty of destruction.

On the 16th of May 1871, the Vendôme Column with the statue of Napoleon I was destroyed by fighters of the Paris Commune. This act of overthrowing power is documented in numerous photographs. Many groups of fighters pose in front of the destroyed monument. What do we learn from such an example, to which many others could be added? We learn that the destruction of a monument is a symbol; a symbol for the will of a society. We, however, preserve and care for the monuments of the past. Sometimes it appears that the rescued statue of a past sovereign compensates for the destruction of entire historical urban quarters. While our society destroys valuable testimonies of the past, it clings to nice little monuments but is unable to create new ones. Historical worship of heroes is certainly not in accordance with our understanding of democracy. But is there nothing left we can believe in? Are we no longer in the position to set signs which, although not useful, can document common sense? Democracy obviously does not stand in need of erecting monuments—but it legitimises itself by testimonies of monarchic and autocratic power. From the monuments which have not been built, we can learn about the self-valuation of a society and what position architecture has in it. *A society which does not believe in its survival is incapable of the symbolic representation of its aim, and therefore incapable of building.*

# ROB KRIER

# ARCHITECTURAL
# COMPOSITION

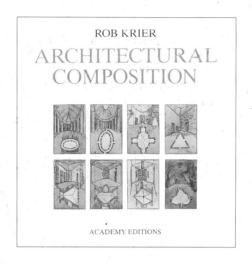

Rob Krier is a unique voice in today's architectural discourse through his commitment to developing a relevant and pragmatic theory of architecture based on his own experience and observations of architectural practice, and opposed to the easy, abstract theorising so common in contemporary architectural writing. Together with his brother Leon, he has perfected a form of presentation in which the potency of his thinking finds its perfect counterpoint in detailed drawings and sketches which argue this visually through the power of example. Following the success of his widely acclaimed *Urban Space*, a work which looked at the problems of our cities from an historical, theoretical and practical standpoint, Krier now applies his particular, highly influential mode of didactic criticism to contemporary architecture in a continuing search for fundamental architectural truths.

*Architectural Composition* is both a theoretical and visual analysis clearly illustrating the creative process which informs Krier's vision and praxis. Separate chapters detail the fundamentals of architectural composition, beginning with function, construction and architectural form; the elements of architecture, including typologies for plans, facades and interior spaces, proportional studies of Gothic cathedrals, the human body, plants, animals and sculpture, demonstrating their reliance on the Golden Section; and a series of critical and discursive essays on the plight of architecture and architects practising today. In addition to his own didactic

illustrations, Krier also draws on student works and photographic examples to support his argument, many of which were commissioned especially for this book. The culmination of years of teaching and practical experience by one of Europe's best known architectural theorists, *Architectural Composition* is without doubt a major achievement, destined to become a standard work of reference for both students and practising architects.

Rob Krier is an architect, educator and influential theorist on architecture and urbanism. He was born in Luxembourg and subsequently emigrated to Austria where he has lived ever since. Krier has produced urban schemes for cities as diverse as Stuttgart, Vienna and Berlin. His built works include extensive social housing schemes in Berlin and more recently projects in Amiens and Vienna. Krier's sculptural work includes six bronzes for the portside of Barcelona (1986), five bronzes for a castle in Luxembourg (1987), a bronze of the philosopher Reuchlin for Pforzheim in Germany (1987), and a pair of figures for the Camillo Sitte Piazza in Vienna (1988) of which he is also the architect. His previous books include *Urban Space*, Academy Editions 1979, and *On Architecture*, Academy Editions (1982). He has been professor at the Technical University of Vienna since 1975.

*250x240 mm, 344 pages including three double gatefolds in colour, over 500 illustrations*                              *ISBN: 0 85670 803 8  Hardback £39.50*

## ACADEMY EDITIONS
### 42 Leinster Gardens, London W2 3AN